PUBLISHER 2002

in eas

STEPHEN COPESTAKE

COMPUTER
STEP

In easy steps is an imprint of Computer Step
Southfield Road . Southam
Warwickshire CV47 0FB . England

http://www.ineasysteps.com

Notice of Liability

Every effort has been made to ensure that this book contains accurate and current information. However, Computer Step and the author shall not be liable for any loss or damage suffered by readers as a result of any information contained herein.

Trademarks

Microsoft® and Windows® are registered trademarks of Microsoft Corporation. All other trademarks are acknowledged as belonging to their respective companies.

Printed and bound in the United Kingdom

ISBN 1-84078-194-7

Contents

Introducing Publisher

Welcome to *Publisher 2002 in easy steps*. This chapter provides a brief introduction to Publisher and the options available to you when you start the program. We also introduce Publisher's star prize – the Publication Wizards. You can then try out some essentials, like navigating through a document, and learn how to use Publisher's Task Pane, handy Smart Tags and Ask-a-Question, the improved replacement for the Office Assistant.

Covers

Chapter One

Starting Publisher

To start Publisher, first click the Start button on the Windows Task bar. Then, move the mouse pointer up the menu options and click on Programs (or All Programs in Windows XP, as here), followed by Microsoft Publisher as illustrated below:

You can start Publisher with fewer actions by creating a Windows shortcut and placing it on the Desktop. See your Windows user guide for instructions.

In the Help menu, Publisher provides the Detect and Repair command to help check and repair non-essential files like fonts and templates.

Publisher provides lots of options for users with disabilities: type 'accessibility' in Ask-a-Question and press Enter to find out more.

To provide the greatest possible amount of useful information, hints and tips about working with Publisher, this book assumes that you're familiar with the basics of Microsoft Windows.

Desktop shortcut

2 Then click here.

3 Finally, click here to start Publisher.

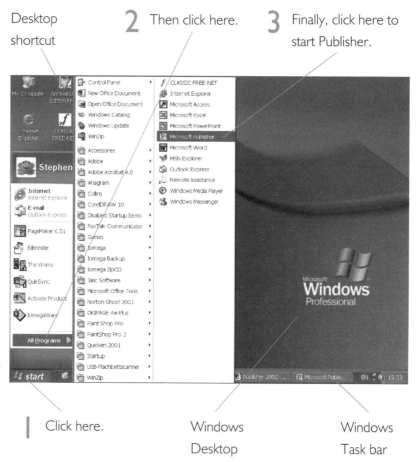

Click here.

Windows Desktop

Windows Task bar

By default, as soon as you click on Publisher 2002 in step 3 above, Publisher displays the New Publication Task Pane – from where you can choose one of the three options shown on the opposite page:

Those who use Microsoft Office will find Publisher is even easier to learn: it follows the Microsoft Office way of doing things.

- You can tell Publisher to create a new publication based on one of the many cleverly designed templates already predesigned for you. This involves using a Publication Wizard, which (initially) asks you some simple questions and then creates the basic layout for you

- Or if you're feeling creative, you can choose the Blank Publications feature, then choose an option from a series of design schemes – and perform the entire page design yourself

- Or you can open an existing Publisher document

To quickly choose a design or style, simply click the desired icon.

5 Click a document type in the list.

4 Click here and select By Design Sets to see the templates organised into design sets. Or select By Blank Publications to see the range of 'blank page' options available.

If you create your own document templates, you can easily gain access to them later by clicking From template.

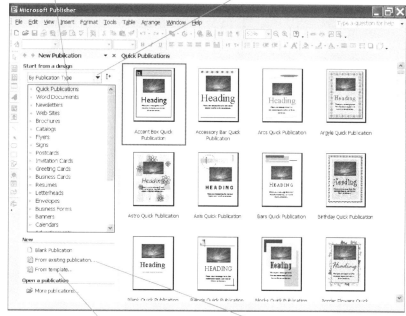

If you're using a version of Windows which predates XP, the screens and dialogs you see will differ somewhat from illustrations shown in this book.

Click here to view any templates that you've made

Click here to display a list of existing Publisher documents

Introducing Publication Wizards

We'll look at opening existing publications and creating your own publications from the beginning later in this book. For now, let's take a brief look at Publication Wizards.

You can use the following method to apply formatting quickly. With the right mouse button, drag an object or text whose formatting you want to copy, onto the object or text where you want to apply the formatting. Release the right mouse button and Publisher displays a floating menu. Choose the Apply Formatting Here command to copy the formatting.

If you choose a Publication Wizard, Publisher does most of the hard work of designing the layout of your publication for you, while still giving you a lot of control over how your publication will eventually look. And remember, even if you've already chosen a Publication Wizard design, you can still edit the design to suit your needs whenever you wish.

So let's imagine you've chosen the Newsletters Publication Wizard. The following dialog box presents you with a range of page designs. Let's examine these below:

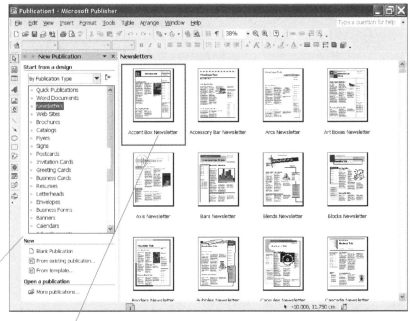

This is one incarnation of Publisher 2002's Task Pane. See page 16 for more information.

Click to select the design you want and launch the wizard.

The Publisher screen

To quickly learn more about a tool on a toolbar, position the mouse pointer directly on top of the desired tool. Publisher then names the tool (ScreenTip) and briefly describes its purpose.

When you start Publisher and choose a document from the Task Pane, or the Blank Publication option, Publisher reveals the Publisher screen. This is where you can create, edit, view, manipulate and save your publication.

The unlabelled elements on the screen are common components of Windows programs. See your Windows documentation for more information.

Another incarnation of Publisher 2002's Task Pane.

Objects toolbar　　Rulers　　Menu bar　　Standard toolbar　　Formatting toolbar　　Title bar

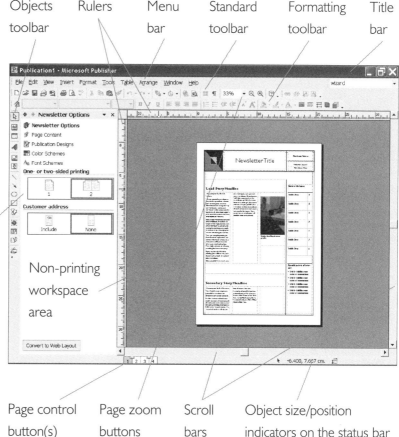

Non-printing workspace area

Page control button(s)　　Page zoom buttons　　Scroll bars　　Object size/position indicators on the status bar

The toolbars, rulers and status bar can be turned on or off by clicking the right mouse button on the non-printing workspace area and choosing the desired option from the menu/submenu.

The toolbars

The Standard, Formatting and Objects toolbars contain buttons to provide quick access to commands. You click a button to gain access to the desired command. When you click on some buttons, Publisher may display other tools or toolbars to extend or customize your choices further.

Selecting

With the Pointer (selection) tool active, you can select several objects at once. Drag a rectangular selection box around the objects you want to select.

In Publisher, you select something if you want to affect the selected item in a particular way. For example, to change the size and proportions of a drawn rectangle, you must select the rectangle first. Only then can you change the height, width, or both, or modify the rectangle.

When you click an object, you select it. Publisher then places selection handles around the selected object:

If you have several objects on the screen, you can keep precise control of which objects you select, by pressing and holding down the SHIFT key as you click objects in sequence.

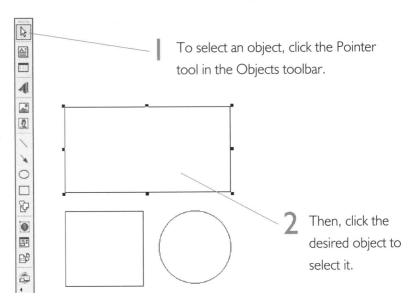

To select an object, click the Pointer tool in the Objects toolbar.

Then, click the desired object to select it.

Sometimes, the desired object may be behind another larger object, making it difficult to select. If this happens, select the largest object (nearest to you), then choose the Order, Send Backward or the Order, Send to Back commands on the Arrange menu.

Selecting all objects

You can select all objects on the Publisher screen in a single action by clicking Select All in the Edit menu. To clear the selection, click anywhere outside of the selection.

If you can't select an object

If the object you want to select does not appear to be selectable, the object may have been placed on the master page. We'll discuss this in detail in Chapter 2; for now, a quick way to move to the master is to press the Ctrl+M keys. This is a shortcut way of choosing the Master Page command in the View menu. Press Ctrl+M again to return to 'normal' (foreground) view.

Moving around a publication

 If your publication is made up of more than a single page, and you're seeing your pages in Single Page view, you can choose to view adjacent pages side by side, by opening the View menu and choosing the Two-Page Spread command.

(Repeating this returns to Single Page view.)

Publisher provides several tools to enable you to move around a publication.

The scroll bars

Click the horizontal or vertical scroll buttons on the horizontal and vertical scroll bars to scroll the publication page up or down, and left or right.

To move quickly, drag the scroll box along the bar, or click a location on the bar representing where you want to go

 If you select an object before you zoom in or out, any following zoom action is centred on the selected object, rather than the entire page.

The page control buttons

To move to a desired page, you can use the page control buttons situated at the lower-most left-hand corner of the Publisher window. See the illustration below:

 You can also use a dialog to move to pages. Press F5. In the Go to page box, type in the relevant page number. Click OK.

In this example, there are 4 pages in the publication

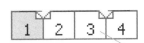

To move to a specific page, simply click the page number you want

The page zoom controls

You can easily move your publication page or selected object closer or further away using the page zoom controls situated on the Standard toolbar (see page 11).

 To quickly switch between the current zoom value and actual page size, press the F9 key. Each time you press F9, the current view toggles.

Click here to display the Zoom options menu

Click here to zoom out

Click here to zoom in

33%

Tracking objects on the workspace

Situated towards the lower right of the Publisher window, the object size and position indicators provide you with the continual feedback that is necessary to place objects accurately on your publication pages.

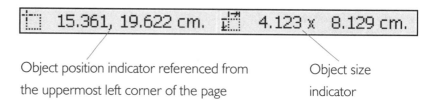

Object position indicator referenced from the uppermost left corner of the page

Object size indicator

If you can't see the object size and position indicators, the Status bar may have been hidden to create more space on the screen. To re-display the Status bar, open the View menu then click Status Bar.

When no object is selected, the object position indicator tracks the mouse pointer. You can change the measurement units used easily, as shown below.

Changing the measurement units

Click the Options command in the Tools menu to display the Options dialog box. Then, in the Options dialog box, you can specify whether to use inches, centimetres, picas or points, as shown in the illustration below.

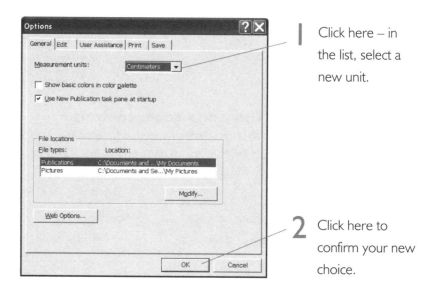

1 Click here – in the list, select a new unit.

2 Click here to confirm your new choice.

Undo and redo

Publisher lets you reverse – 'undo' – just about any editing operation. If, subsequently, you decide that you do want to proceed with an operation that you've reversed, you can 'redo' it.

You can even undo or redo a series of operations in one go.

You can undo and redo actions in the following ways (in descending order of complexity):

- via the keyboard

- from within the Edit menu

- from within the Standard toolbar

To redo an action, do the following on the Standard toolbar:

Click here; in the list, select one or more redo actions

Using the keyboard
Simply press Ctrl+Z to undo an action, or Ctrl+Y to reinstate it.

Using the Edit menu
Pull down the Edit menu and click Undo... or Redo... as appropriate (the ellipses denote the precise nature of the action to be reversed or reinstated).

Using the Standard toolbar
Carry out the following action to undo an action (see the DON'T FORGET tip for how to reinstate it):

Click here.

Re step 2 – if you select an early operation in the list (i.e. one near the bottom), all later operations are included.
  (This applies to Redo, too.)

2 Select 1 or more operations.

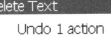

Delete Text
Undo 1 action

Publisher's Task Pane

Publisher 2002 provides a special pane on the left of the screen which you can use to launch various tasks or apply specific formatting. There are various incarnations of the Task Pane, depending on which task you're performing. For example, the main ones are:

- New Publication
- Clipboard
- Search
- Insert Clip Art

There are also specific formatting versions which are discussed later.

Using the Task Pane

To display or hide the Task Pane, pull down the View menu and click Task Pane.

Publisher's menus automatically update so that they show those program features you use most often.

To make a menu display all its features, click the chevron – – at the base.

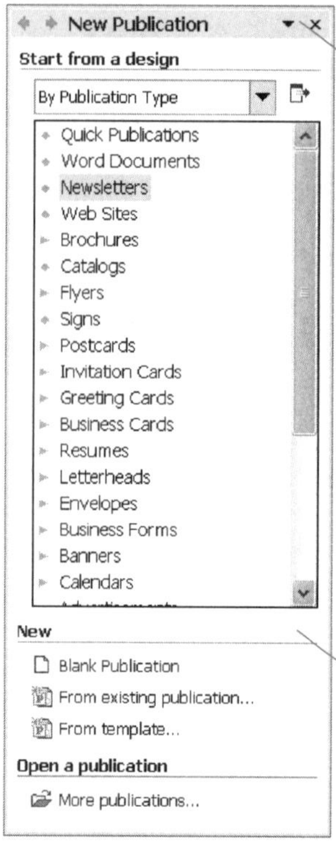

To select a new Task Pane, click here – in the menu, click an entry.

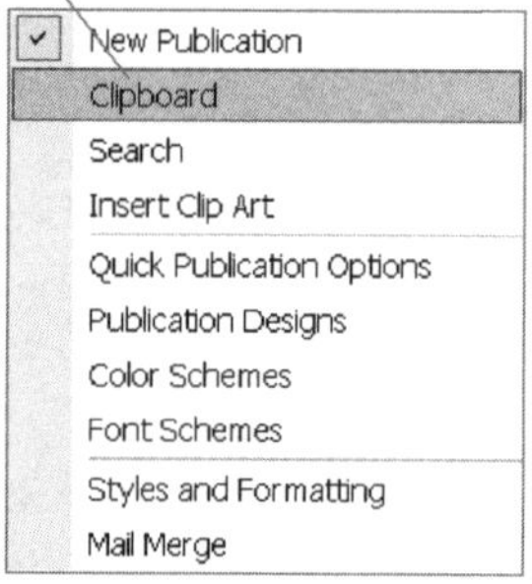

This is the New Publication Task Pane

Using Smart Tags

Publisher 2002 recognises certain types of data and highlights them in various ways e.g. by applying a small blue box. When you move the mouse pointer over the text, an 'action button' appears which provides access to commands which would otherwise have to be accessed from menus/toolbars or other programs.

The Paste Options button

Re step 2 – choose Keep Source Formatting to retain the pasted text's original format.

'Button' has been copied and the Paste command (Shift+Insert) issued...

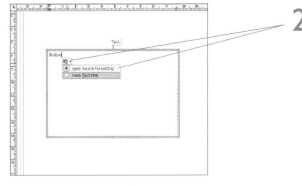

Here, text has been entered into Publisher text frames (see chapter 5 and elsewhere for more on text frames)

2 Clicking the arrow launches a menu – make a choice.

The AutoCorrect button

An AutoCorrect entry has been set up which replaces 'ws' with 'was'.

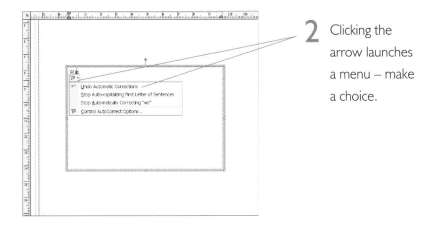

2 Clicking the arrow launches a menu – make a choice.

Ask-a-Question

In Publisher 2000, users had to run the Office Assistant (see the tip) to get answers to plain-English questions. In Publisher 2002, however, this isn't the case. Simply do the following:

In Publisher 2002, the Office Assistant is turned off by default. To turn it on, pull down the Help menu and click Show the Office Assistant.

The Assistant is an animated (and frequently unpopular) helper which answers questions, but you can achieve the same effect more easily with Ask-a-Question. (This is the method Microsoft recommends.)

Type in your question here and press Enter.

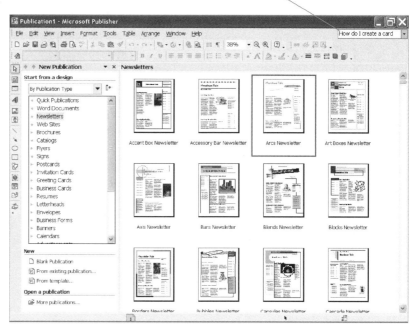

○ Create a card

○ Create a Mail Merge

○ Create an invitation

○ Repeat text and pictures on facing pages

○ Work with text styles

○ None of the above, search for more on the Web

2 Click a relevant entry or See more (if available) for more topics.

Getting started with the basics

In this chapter, we examine how to start, open and close a publication in Publisher. We also explore how to customise publications with design sets, and look at creating and manipulating frames, a technique which is central to the use of Publisher 2002. You'll also create multiple linked text frames and flow text between them.

Finally, we'll examine the use of Publisher's Master page as a handy way to insert objects (e.g. watermarks) on all pages within a publication.

Covers

Chapter Two

Starting a new publication

After starting Publisher, the quickest way to create a publication might be to use a Publication Wizard as discussed in chapter 1. However, if you want to start a new publication based entirely on your own design and creativity, follow step 1 below in the New Publication Task Pane to see a range of publication templates.

As you can see below, Publisher provides several blank page options by presetting the margins and page size for the type of blank page publication you choose:

Once you've decided on the type of publication you want, if you're going to use an outside printing service to print your final publication, you need to establish your printing options now – before adding any design components to your page.

For how to do this, see chapter 13.

To tell Publisher not to display the New Publication Task Pane each time you start Publisher, choose Options from the Tools menu. Click the General tab then untick Use New Publication task pane at startup. Finally, click OK.

Click here – in the list, select By Blank Publications.

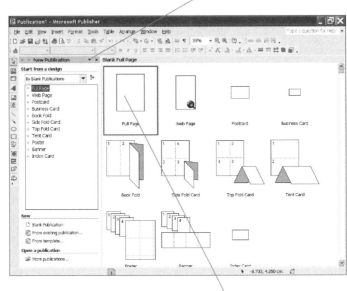

2 To select a template, click the desired template icon.

Establishing your target printer

After you've decided the type of publication you want to create, next you must tell Publisher the name of the printer to which you intend to print your final publication. The choice of printer affects the size of the printable area on your page, the page sizes available, margin widths, fonts available to your publication, and so on. Therefore, this must be done soon after you start your publication.

You can set your target printer by first opening the File menu and clicking the Page Setup command to display the Page Setup dialog box. Then perform the following steps:

1 Click the Printer & Paper tab.

Page Setup

Layout | Printer & Paper

Printer
Name: Epson Stylus COLOR ESC/P 2 | Properties
Type: Epson Stylus COLOR ESC/P 2
Where: LPT1:
Comment:

Preview

Paper
Size: A4
Source: Automatically Select

Orientation
A
○ Portrait
○ Landscape

OK | Cancel

3 (Optional) Click here to change the standard settings already established for your desired printer.

If, after laying out your publication, you change your target printer, when you print your publication it may not look as you intended: fonts may be missing or substituted, and page sizes and margins may differ.

2 Click here; in the list, select a printer for use as your target printer (if you're using an outside printer, see below).

4 Click here to confirm your options.

Using an outside print shop

If you're going to use external word-processed files and clip art in your publication, now is a good time to make sure you have these ready and available for Publisher to use.

If you plan to use a commercial print shop to print your final publication, you'll need to establish the setup now before adding design components to your pages. This aspect is covered in depth in chapter 13.

Many print organizations now accept Publisher files, without any conversion needed by you. This can obviously ensure your publishing task is easier and can indeed save you money. Key point: find a reliable print shop that can demonstrate a track record of working with Publisher files. Ideally, get personal recommendations from friends, colleagues or business contacts before making your choice.

Opening a publication

In earlier versions of Publisher, you could have only one publication open at any one time. Publisher 2002, however, allows multiple open publications.

To open an existing publication, choose the Open command in the File menu (or press the Ctrl+O keys). Then perform the following steps:

To quickly display the Open Publication dialog box, click the Open button:

on the Standard toolbar.

Publisher keeps track of the four most recently opened Publisher files and stores their names at the bottom of the File menu. To quickly open any one of these files, click the desired file name.

Locate and select the file you want to open.

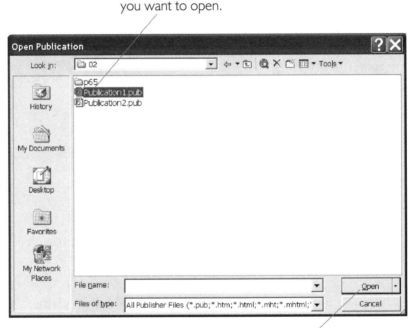

2 Click Open.

Opening a Publisher document from the New Publication Task Pane

In the New Publication Task Pane, click From existing publication. Complete the dialog which launches (it's almost the same as the illustration above).

Using Publication Design Sets

From chapter 1, we can see that when you start Publisher, it automatically displays the New Publication Task Pane. Remember, you can open an existing Publisher document, create an entirely new one using your own settings, or use a Publication Wizard to help make some important choices for you.

If you decide to create a new publication using a Wizard, you can make your choice based on publication type – like newsletter or brochure – or if you want your publication to match other types of publications, you can create a publication based on specific design elements by choosing By Design Sets in the New Publication Task Pane. In this way you can ensure your newsletter, for example, uses a design style and colour scheme that matches your stationery, brochures and business cards, and so on:

Publisher 2002 supports even more professionally created design sets.

You can apply design sets to existing publications. Click here: and select Publication Designs in the menu. In the Publication Designs Task Pane, do the following:

Click here; in the list, select By Design Sets.

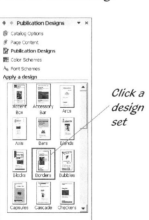

Click a design set

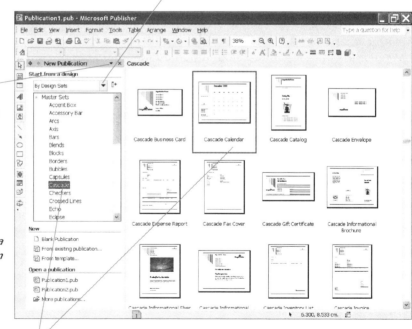

2 Choose your desired design set and click a particular design to apply it.

A frame for every object

To drag a ruler onto the page, simply place the mouse pointer on a ruler; it changes to a double arrow symbol. Drag the desired ruler on to the page. When finished, simply drag the ruler back to its origin.

Introducing objects

Until now, we've referred to objects in the general sense. However, in Publisher, the term 'object' has a more precise meaning. An object is simply any independently movable item which you can place and move about on the workspace – for example, a text block, table, or piece of clip art. Objects are examined in more detail in chapter 3.

Introducing frames

WordArt is a program which is available in Publisher if you want to apply some fancy effects to text using different font styles and so on. For example, you can wrap text around a shape, or curve text like this:

Publisher uses frames to 'hold' objects to make the job of moving objects around easier. These objects include:

- Text

- Pictures

- Tables

- WordArt

- Clip art

Although frames are crucial to the use of these objects, the user is often unaware of them.

All frames can be resized, moved and aligned precisely using guidelines and ruler marks, and even aligned to other objects.

See page 26 for how to use the rotation handle.

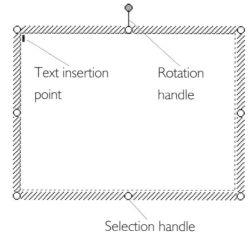

Text insertion point

Rotation handle

An empty (but selected) text block/ frame with the rotation handle flagged

Selection handle

Creating text/picture frames

You can also create table frames manually – see the HOT TIP below.

You create most Publisher objects directly, and the appropriate frames are created automatically. However, there are a few exceptions. You can create text and picture frames manually.

Creating picture frames

To insert text frames/blocks, click this button:
Now do one of the following:

- *Drag out a text frame/ block with the mouse.*
- *Click where you want to enter text – Publisher inserts a square block for you*

Begin entering text. (If you want to zoom in to the frame, press the F9 key.)

The insertion of other objects is covered later in this book, at the following locations:

- *WordArt objects – page 89.*
- *Clip art and pictures – page 112 and pages 119–120 respectively.*
- *Tables – pages 98–99.*

Click the Picture Frame button in the Objects toolbar.

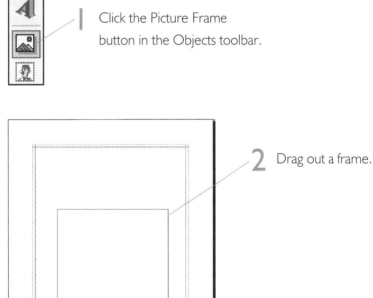

2 Drag out a frame.

3 In the Insert Picture dialog, locate and double-click the picture you want to insert in the frame.

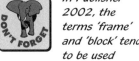

In Publisher 2002, the terms 'frame' and 'block' tend to be used more or less interchange-ably.

Manipulating frames

You can resize a frame by changing its width, height, or both width and height at the same time. To keep the original frame proportions, press and hold down the Shift key while you resize a frame using a corner selection handle. Or, if you want to keep the centre of the frame in the original position, use the Ctrl key instead. Alternatively, use both techniques at once.

To change frame width

1 Hold down the mouse button on the left or right selection handle.

2 Drag the mouse towards the left or towards the right.

To change frame height

1 Hold down the mouse button on the top-middle, or bottom-middle selection handle.

2 Drag the mouse upwards or downwards only until you see the desired height.

To rotate a frame, drag its Rotation handle to the left or right:

To change height and width at the same time

1 Hold down the mouse button on any corner selection handle.

2 Drag diagonally until you see the desired size.

To move a frame

1 Hold down the mouse button anywhere on the perimeter but not on a selection handle.

2 Drag to the new location.

To delete an empty frame

1 Click inside the frame you want to delete.

2 Press the Delete key.

Flowing text

Once text has been flowed into multiple frames, you can easily follow the 'flow' from one frame to the next simply by clicking the Go To Next Frame and Go To Previous Frame buttons.

You can bring text into Publisher in the following ways. You can:

- Type directly into a text block (see page 25).

- Copy text from another program or file.

- Import an entire text file from another program.

- Import direct from some versions of Microsoft Word.

- Link or embed text using OLE.

Where you have multiple connected text frames, if you want to disconnect a text frame from the others, first click in any connected text frame (other than the last in the sequence), then choose this button on the Standard toolbar:

Each of these methods will be discussed as we come to them, but for now let's assume you've drawn a text block. You can then start typing text directly into it:

You can begin typing straightaway. As you enter a line of text, Publisher 2002 automatically starts a new line. And so on…

1 The Text Overflow symbol (A•••) appears when there's more text in the frame than can currently be viewed. To flow the remaining hidden text, first draw another text frame.

Often, you'll want to flow text into a frame which is situated on another page. In this situation, it's helpful to have Publisher insert 'Continue on page XX' and 'Continued from page XX' labels.

Right-click a linked text box. In the menu, select Format Text Box. In the dialog, select the Text Box tab. Tick Include "Continued on page…" and/or Include "Continued from page…". Click OK.

2 Click back in the first block. Click the Connect Text Box Link button on the Standard toolbar:

3 The mouse pointer then changes into a cup symbol: Click in the text block where you want to place the excess text from the first text frame.

4 Publisher 'pours' the remaining text into the second block; it places a Go To Next Frame button at the bottom of the first text block and a Go To Previous Frame button at the top of this frame. Note: the Go To … buttons are only visible in the block containing the text cursor.

The Master page

In Publisher, you can place objects that are the same from page to page – like logos and page numbers – on the Master. All other objects are placed on the foreground.

The Master is ideal for placing watermarks or similar repeating lightly-shaded design elements.

By default, when you're working on a publication, you're actually working on the foreground. So although you can see any objects placed on the Master, you cannot directly affect Master objects.

To work on the Master, you must switch to Master view. You can then work on the Master page in the same way as you do with any other page in Publisher. To switch to Master view, do the following:

Repeat step 1 to return to foreground view.

Pull down the View menu and click Master Page.

The Master page looks exactly the same as foreground view (except it's likely to be emptier.)

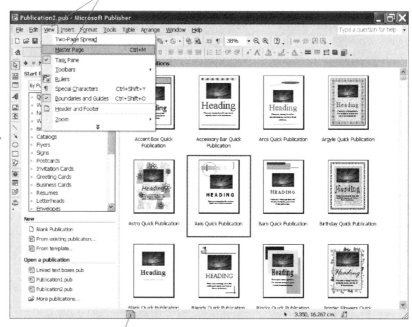

You can quickly establish whether you're viewing the Master or the foreground. Simply look at the page buttons situated at the lower left of the screen; if you can see 1 or more page numbers, then you're in foreground view.

Saving your publication

It's a good idea to save often. With important publications, ideally save at least every 10 minutes.

After establishing a publication's basic layout, it's a good time to save it. Click the Save button on the Standard toolbar:

or open the File menu, then click Save to display the Save As dialog box:

| Choose where you want to store your publication.

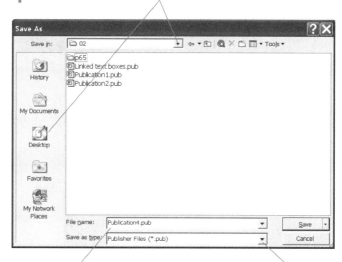

Once you've named a publication, you can avoid using the menus or toolbar and simply press CTRL+S, if you wish. This makes saving a lot quicker.

2 Name your publication.

3 (Optional) If you use the same style of publication often, you could save it as a template: click here and choose Publisher Template.

4 Click the Save button. Or click the arrow to the right of the button and select Save with Backup to also create a backup version.

After you've saved your publication once, the next time you save, Publisher already knows the filename and so will not display the Save As dialog box again (unless you choose to save your publication to another name by clicking the Save As command in the File menu).

Closing Publisher

Closing your publication

To close the current Publisher document, open the File menu and click the Close command. If the document you've been working on has not been saved, Publisher displays the following message:

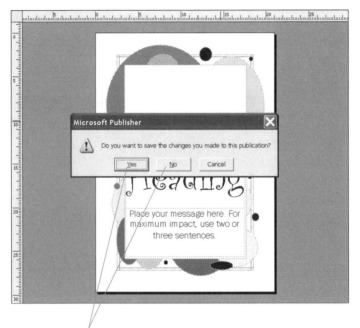

Click Yes to save or click No to close
the current publication without saving

At this stage, whether you choose to save or not to save, Publisher clears the current publication from the screen and replaces it with a new blank page. You can then start a new publication, open an existing document, or exit Publisher.

Ending a Publisher session

To exit Publisher, click on the Exit command in the File menu. If you have an open publication when you choose the Exit command, Publisher closes the document before exiting the program.

If you've finished your current Publisher session, but still have other programs running, you can provide more memory for the other programs by exiting Publisher.

Working with text/graphic objects

Objects are an important concept in Publisher. In this chapter, we discover commands and techniques that enable you to arrange and manipulate objects, to create some really stunning effects.

Covers

Chapter Three

Using the Format Painter

Remember, you can copy a selected object using the Copy and Paste commands in the Edit menu, or from the pop-up menu when you right-click on a selected object. However, sometimes you may only want to copy the formatting of an object, not the object itself. Publisher provides a quick and easy way to do this. Select the object whose formatting you want to copy, then carry out the steps below:

You can also use the Format Painter to copy text formatting from one text object to another. First, click in the text frame whose formatting you want to copy. Then perform the steps described on this page.

1 On the Standard toolbar, click the Format Painter button.

2 As you move the mouse pointer back onto the page, the mouse pointer symbol changes to a Paintbrush:

There's another way to quickly copy formatting from one object to another. With the right mouse button, drag the object whose formatting you want to copy onto the target object. Then click Apply Formatting Here in the menu.

3 To copy the formatting of the selected object to another single object, click the desired target object. If you want to copy the formatting to several objects, click-and-drag a selection box around the objects to which you want to copy formatting. When you release the mouse pointer, Publisher copies the formatting to the objects you specified.

Moving objects

Moving one or more objects in Publisher is simple. You may want to move objects around the page, from the page to the workspace, and from page to page. To move an object, perform the following steps:

You cannot move highlighted text using this technique, as highlighted text is not an object. However, you can use the Cut and Paste commands instead.

1 Click the object you want to move. Publisher then places selection handles around the object.

3 When the mouse pointer symbol changes to the Mover symbol, drag the object to the desired location.

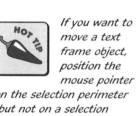

If you want to move a text frame object, position the mouse pointer on the selection perimeter (but not on a selection handle). The Mover symbol will not appear inside a text block object.

4 Release the left mouse button.

2 Place the mouse pointer over the selected object or on the object's perimeter (but not on a selection handle).

Moving several objects at a time

The workspace area surrounding the paper is an ideal place to store objects temporarily.

One way to move several objects together is to hold down Shift as you click each object you want to move, and move the mouse pointer over the selection until the Mover symbol appears, then drag to the new location as described above. To constrain the movement to the horizontal or vertical directions only, continue holding down Shift until the objects are in the new position and you have released the mouse button.

Resizing objects

To resize using the object centre as the reference point, hold down Ctrl while you drag a corner selection handle. But release the mouse button before you release Ctrl.

You can easily change the size of any single object or group of objects at any time. When you resize a group of objects, Publisher can temporarily configure the group as a single object. Carry out the following steps to resize objects:

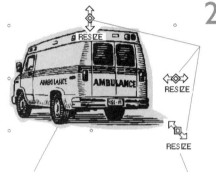

To constrain the resizing action both proportionally and centrally, hold down both Shift and Ctrl keys as you resize, but release the mouse button before you release Shift and Ctrl.

2 Place the mouse pointer over a selection handle, and:

- to change the height, use the middle top or bottom selection handle;
- to change the width, use the middle left or right handle;
- to change both height and width at the same time, use a corner handle.

1 Click the object you want to resize. Publisher then places selection handles around the object.

3 When the mouse pointer symbol changes to a RESIZE symbol, drag to resize the object to the desired size.

When you've selected items to move or resize by dragging, remember, you can also right-click the selection to display commands for manipulating objects.

To resize a text frame or custom shape keeping to the original proportions, hold down the Shift key as you resize, but release the mouse button before you release Shift. To resize a picture in the same way, simply perform the action in step 3 above.

Resizing a group of objects

To resize several objects at the same time, hold down Shift while you click each object you want to resize. Next, click the Group Objects button at the lower right corner of the selection:

To align an object on the page, select it. Choose Align or Distribute in the Arrange menu. In the submenu, select an option e.g. Align Center or Align Bottom.

Then, perform steps 2 to 3 above and resize as desired. Finally, click the Group Objects button again to ungroup the objects.

Positioning objects precisely

You can position a selected object precisely: first zoom in to the desired object, then hold down Alt while you press the Up, Down, Left or Right cursor keys.

You can also move objects in small steps by 'nudging' them. In the Arrange menu, select Nudge. In the submenu, click Up, Down, Left or Right.

(To change the Nudge distance, choose Tools, Options. Select the Edit tab. Tick Arrow keys nudge objects by: and enter a new value in the data box. Click OK.)

Ruler guides can help you position an object precisely. To drag a ruler guide onto the page, hold down Shift while you place the mouse pointer on the horizontal or vertical ruler. When the mouse pointer changes to the 'Adjust' symbol, drag a guide onto the page.

We saw earlier (page 26) how to rotate frames/objects with the mouse. Sometimes, however, this procedure may not provide the precision you need. To rotate an object to a precise angle, right-click the object. In the menu, select the Format option (the precise wording varies according to the object selected). Do the following:

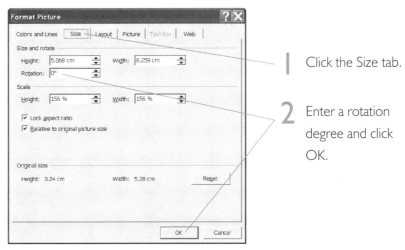

1 Click the Size tab.

2 Enter a rotation degree and click OK.

Using 'Snap to...'

Publisher uses the term 'snap' to mean 'pull towards something'. The Arrange menu contains the three commands listed below. These can also be used to help align text and graphic objects on the page. When these commands are turned on, Publisher places a tick mark next to the command. To turn the command off, simply click the command on the menu.

Snap, To Ruler Marks	Drag the object you want to the desired location as described previously in this chapter, until the edge of the object snaps to the desired ruler mark.
Snap, To Guides	Works in the same way as Snap to Ruler Marks, except you snap to the desired guide.
Snap, To Objects	Drag an object towards the object to which you want to snap. When within snapping range, Publisher snaps the selected object to the destination object.

Mirroring an object

Rotating objects with the mouse is covered on page 26, and precise rotation on page 35.

Publisher provides a wide range of tools to help you create attractive and interesting publications. For example, sometimes you may want to create an eye-catching effect by including two objects which display as mirror images of each other. You can easily create a mirror image of any shape or line created with the drawing tools, or inserted clip art. You can also 'flip' objects.

Flipping in action

You can flip an object horizontally or vertically. Carry out the following steps to 'flip' a desired object or multiple selected objects:

You can also use this technique as another way to rotate objects. In step 2, select a preset rotation (e.g. Rotate Left) to rotate by 90°.

1 Select the relevant object(s).

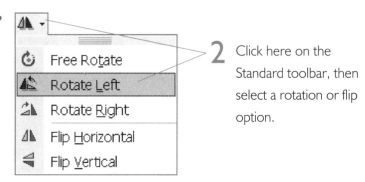

2 Click here on the Standard toolbar, then select a rotation or flip option.

Unflipped picture

Flip Horizontal

Flip Vertical

Grouping and ungrouping objects

Sometimes, you may want to work with several objects at the same time, without disturbing the position or spacing of the individual objects in relation to each other. Wouldn't it be great if these objects could be treated as a single item while you move, resize or rotate the group in a single action? You can do this in Publisher using a procedure known as grouping.

To group and ungroup several objects, do the following:

Another way to select objects you want to group is to press and hold down the Shift key while you click on them individually.

1 Hold down the left mouse button and drag a selection box around the objects you want to group.

Even though objects may be grouped, you can still change the border, shading or text of any individual object. First, hold down Ctrl as you click the grouped object you want to affect. Then choose the desired command.

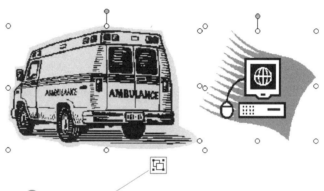

2 Click the Group Objects button.

To identify at a glance if an object is grouped, look at the selection handles. Grouped objects have one set of selection handles around the group.

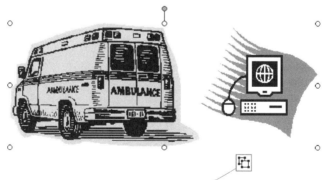

3 To ungroup the selection, select it then click the button again.

4 Click anywhere outside the selection.

Layering objects

You can also change the layering of more than one object at a time, by first selecting all the objects you want to change. (To do this, hold down the Shift key while you click each object you want.)

To create the illusion of depth, you can place several overlapping objects on a page. The last object placed appears to be closest to the viewer, while the first object placed seems furthest away, and so on. Publisher refers to this condition as layering, and we refer to the layered objects collectively as the 'stack'.

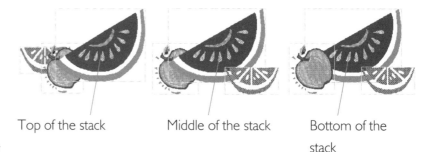

Top of the stack   Middle of the stack   Bottom of the stack

To ensure text or pictures appear behind all objects on every page in your publication, place the objects you want on the Master (see page 28).

Changing the order of layered objects

1   Click the object you want to change.

2   Open the Arrange menu and select Order. Now choose one of the following commands, depending on what you want to do:

To overlay text onto another object, drag out a text frame, type and format your text, then place it in front of the object. Arrange the order of layering. To see the object through the text frame, select the text frame and toggle the Ctrl+T keys.

- Bring to Front
- Bring Forward
- Send Backward
- Send to Back

Applying and changing borders

To delete a border entirely, first click the object whose border you want to delete. Next, click the Line/Border Style button on the Formatting toolbar. Finally, click the None command on the floating menu.

Borders are great for making a picture stand out, or teasing the eye towards an object, or even as design elements in their own right. You can easily add, modify or delete a border around a text or graphic object. Furthermore, with rectangular borders, you can change the colour and thickness of the individual sides. Therefore, to add a border around an object, first click the object to select it. Then carry out the steps below:

1. On the Formatting toolbar, click the Line/Border Style button:

Publisher applies a border inside a frame. Therefore, avoid making the thickness of a border too wide. If a border is too wide, graphic objects may become compressed or some text in a text frame may become hidden.

2. You can quickly apply a border simply by clicking the desired line on the floating menu.

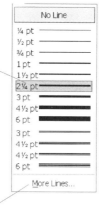

3. Alternatively, you can see more borders by clicking More Lines.

Before step 4, select the Colors and Lines tab.

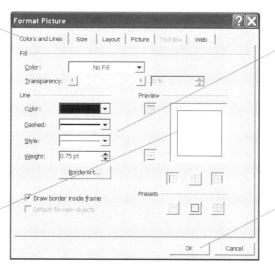

4. Complete the fields here e.g. select a colour and specify whether it's dashed.

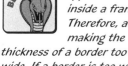

To change an individual side of a border, click the side you want here after step 3. Then optionally perform step 4. Finally, carry out step 5.

5. Click OK.

Making an object transparent

Another way in which you can add interest, contrast and sparkle to a document is to change the default fill of objects. In Publisher, all objects you create – including frames – have a default fill status. Usually this is set to 'transparent'. You can build up a design that is perhaps made up of several individually drawn elements containing various fill colours, tints and pattern styles. Sometimes, you can further enhance a design by selectively making objects transparent, as shown below:

If the apply transparent/ opaque operation does not appear to work, you may be trying to work on an image imported from another application. The action works only with objects which originate in Publisher.

If your document may be used as part of a website, think carefully about applying a pattern or gradient fill to a text frame. When you publish to the web, Publisher converts this type of text frame to a graphic; it will take longer for users to download.

1 Select the object you want to make transparent (here, the banner text).

2 Press Ctrl+T, to switch the state. Each time you press Ctrl+T, the state toggles.

If you apply Ctrl+T to a piece of selected clip art, only the clip art background transparent/opaque status is changed, not the clip art itself. Some attractive designs can be created using this technique.

Several objects can be affected at once by holding down Shift while you click each object you want to make transparent. Alternatively, draw a selection box around all the objects you want to change to select the entire group, then apply the steps above.

Making an object opaque

Making an object opaque is of course simply the reverse of making an object transparent, except that you have a choice of which style of opaqueness – or fill – to apply. You can change various attributes, including the colour of the fill and the pattern.

To make an object opaque and apply a fill, carry out the following steps:

For more detailed information on applying fills/ patterns, see pages 52–53.

To quickly make a transparent selected object opaque, and apply the default fill, simply press Ctrl+T.

Here, a two-colour fill (with vertical shading) has been applied.

2 Click the arrow on the Fill Color button on the Formatting toolbar:

3 On the Colors Palette, click on the colour you want to apply.

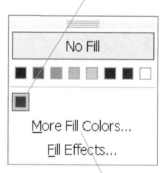

1 Select the transparent object you want to make opaque.

4 Or, to see more colour choices, click More Fill Colors, then click your desired colour followed by the OK button.

5 To apply a shade, tint, pattern or gradient, click the Fill Effects button, then click the desired options followed by the OK button.

Applying a shadow

Shadows in Publisher enhance the illusion of depth and can transform a plain shape into something more striking. You can apply a shadow to any shape created with the drawing tools or around any frames. To add further specialist shadowed effects to text, you can use the WordArt program that comes with Publisher. To shadow an object, perform the following steps:

You can also shadow text itself (rather than its frame) via another technique:

1 Click the object to select it.

Select the text. Pull down the Format menu and click Font. In the Effects section of the Font dialog, tick Shadow. Click OK.

2 On the Formatting toolbar, click this icon:

4 The object with shadow applied.

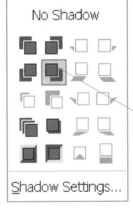

3 Click a shadow.

To customise a shadow, click Shadow Settings in step 3. Do the following:

Click any of these to nudge the shadow to the size/position you want

Removing an applied shadow

You can remove a shadow by selecting No Shadow in step 3 above.

Using Object Linking & Embedding

Not all programs are OLE-compatible. To view a list of all programs on your system that are OLE-compatible, click Object in the Insert menu, and use the scroll bar to view the contents of the Object Type box.

Objects can be created in other programs and included ('embedded') in a Publisher document. For example, you might want to use a chart created in Microsoft Excel. Furthermore, a linked object maintains a link to its original source program. Often, the information used to form these objects may change, and so you need a method to make sure these objects can be updated easily, even if already placed in a Publisher document. The answer is provided by an enhancement called Object Linking and Embedding (OLE), which may be included in the software.

OLE ensures that if any such objects are placed within a Publisher document, you can start up the source program from within Publisher (by double-clicking the object's icon) to edit the object using the tools from the source program – without leaving Publisher. For this to work, however, you must first link or embed the desired object in a Publisher document, and also, the source program must be OLE-compatible.

Linking or embedding an object

Embed an object when you're the only person working on the publication, so that any changes you make to the contents of an embedded object affect only that publication.

To link or embed an object, first make sure no other object is selected in Publisher. Then carry out the steps below:

1 Open the Insert menu and click the Object command.

2 Click Create from File.

Link an object if you're sharing it with other people or other documents. Then, any changes made to the content of the object can be reflected wherever that object exists.

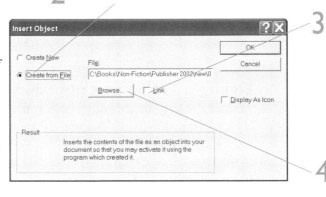

3 To embed an object, jump to step 4. To link an object, click here first.

4 Click here.

5 In the Browse dialog box, navigate through the folders to find the file you want to link/embed, and click that file to select it. Click the Open button.

6 Click OK.

After Publisher has created the new linked or embedded object, you can move and resize the object as described earlier in this chapter.

Updating a linked object

To update the link to an object in your publication, first open the Edit menu and click Links. Then carry out the steps below:

1 In the list of linked objects, click the object you want to update.

4 Click Close.

To change a link, first open the Edit menu and click Links. Next, in the list of linked objects, click the object whose link you want to change. Click the Change Source button then locate and select the file to which you want to link. Finally, click OK, followed by Close.

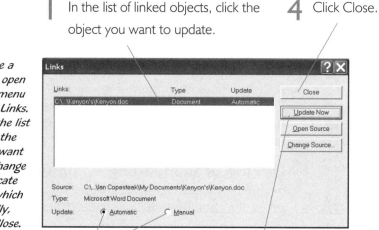

2 Click either Automatic or Manual for the method of update.

3 Click Update Now. If the object is already up-to-date, this button may be shown greyed-out (unavailable).

Editing a linked or embedded object

To edit a linked or embedded object, first double-click the desired object. Next, make your changes using the source program's tools. To return to Publisher, click the Exit or Exit and Return command in the source program's File menu, followed by clicking Yes if prompted to save. However, if you can only see the Publisher Title bar, simply click outside the object workspace to return to Publisher proper.

Drawing simple shapes

This chapter explores how you can create and modify lines, rectangles, circles and other simple geometrical shapes using the drawing tools in the Objects toolbar. You can also discover how to border objects; create more complex shapes known as AutoShapes; and change fill colours/patterns.

Finally, you'll convert shapes into 3D.

Covers

Chapter Four

Working with lines and arrows

Lines can help give emphasis to, and separate, information within a document. In Publisher you can choose from a range of line styles and types, from plain lines and arrowhead lines to fancy lines – which are lines made up of individual elements using the Border Style dialog box. To draw a simple line, perform the steps below:

1 Click the Line tool: on the Objects toolbar.

2 Place the mouse pointer where you want the line to begin and drag the mouse to create the desired line length.

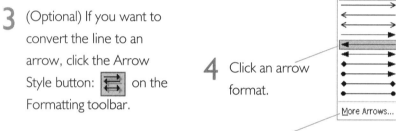

3 (Optional) If you want to convert the line to an arrow, click the Arrow Style button: on the Formatting toolbar.

4 Click an arrow format.

5 (Optional) If you want to choose a different line style or see further arrow options, click More Arrows.

To create a fancy line, first draw a narrow box with the Box tool. Then click the Line/Border Style button on the Formatting toolbar, followed by the More Lines command. Click the Colors and Lines tab, then the BorderArt button. Choose your desired border settings and click OK twice.

To draw a straight line precisely, hold down the Shift key while you draw the line. Or press the Ctrl key to draw a straight line precisely from the centre outwards.

6 Complete these fields, as appropriate.

7 Click OK.

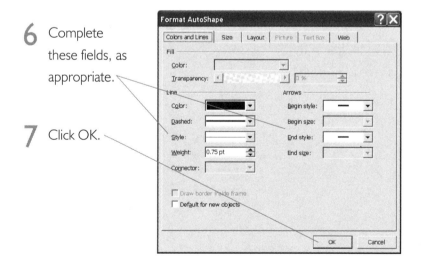

Drawing a rectangle

The box or rectangle shape is one of the most common components used in page design. You can draw rectangles easily using the Rectangle tool on the Objects toolbar. To draw a simple rectangle, carry out the following steps:

To draw a precise square, hold down the Shift key as you drag the mouse diagonally.

1 Click the Rectangle tool: on the Objects toolbar.

2 Place the mouse pointer where you want the uppermost left corner to start, then drag down diagonally towards the right.

3 When you see the desired box shape, release the mouse button.

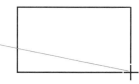

To draw a rectangle from the centre outwards, hold down the Ctrl key as you drag the mouse diagonally.

Drawing a fancy rectangle

To create a more striking box with a fancy border, first right-click inside the existing box. Then do the following:

1 Click Format AutoShape in the menu. In the Format AutoShape dialog, select the Colors and Lines tab. Click the Border Art button.

2 Click a new border style.

3 Click the OK button to make your changes.

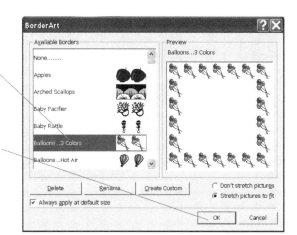

To draw a precise square from the centre outwards, hold down both the Shift and Ctrl keys as you drag the mouse diagonally.

Drawing an oval/circle

Any shape you create with the drawing tools is an object. Therefore, you can change the size and proportion of any drawn shape by dragging the selection handles.

The Measurement toolbar can help you create and position objects precisely. To display the Measurement toolbar, right-click on any empty space on the Desktop and choose Toolbars, Measurement.

To verify whether this technique has worked, pull down the File menu and click Print Preview – part of the object should be invisible.

An excerpt from Print Preview

Press Esc to leave Print Preview.
If no part of the object was invisible, select the text box and press Ctrl+T.

You can draw any variety of oval shape or a precise circle using the Oval tool on the Objects toolbar. Carry out the following steps to draw an oval or circle:

1 Click the Oval tool on the Objects toolbar:

2 Place the mouse pointer at the location where you want the upper-left of the oval or circle to be, then drag down diagonally. To draw a perfect circle, hold down the Shift key as you drag the mouse.

3 When you see the desired shape, release the mouse button.

As with any shape you create with the drawing tools, you can change the outline colour, type and size, in addition to changing the object fill. These aspects are examined later in this chapter. But for now, let's take a quick look at how you can hide part of a drawn oval (or any other object).

Hiding part of an oval (or any other object)

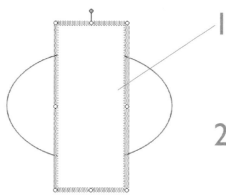

1 With the Text tool, draw a shape directly on top of the oval, so that it covers the part you want hidden.

2 Click outside of the selection to hide the selection handles.

3 When you print, both the text frame and the hidden part of the object will not be seen.

Using AutoShapes

AutoShapes represent an extraordinarily flexible and easy-to-use way to insert a wide variety of shapes into your publications. Once inserted, they can be:

- resized

- rotated/flipped

Inserting an AutoShape

Do the following:

1 Click the AutoShapes tool on the Objects toolbar:

2 Select a category.

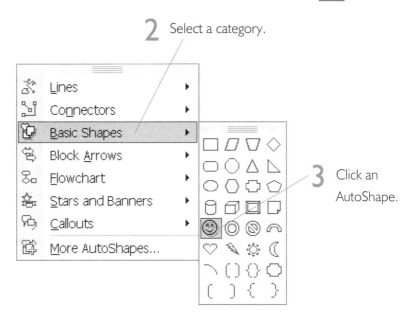

3 Click an AutoShape.

Re step 5 – hold down Shift as you drag to maintain the original height/width relationship.

4 Place the mouse pointer where you want your AutoShape to start.

5 Using the left mouse button, drag out the shape.

Resizing AutoShapes

Select the AutoShape. Now do the following:

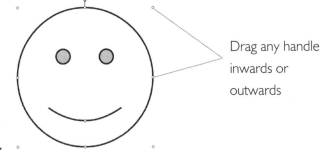

Drag any handle
inwards or
outwards

*You can make
some
AutoShapes
3D. Select the
AutoShape
then click this button in the
Formatting toolbar:*

*In the menu, select a 3D
shape (or No 3-D to restore
it to 2D).*

Access to more AutoShapes

To access additional AutoShapes, follow step 1 on page 49. In 2,
however, click More AutoShapes.

*A 2D shape
converted
to 3D*

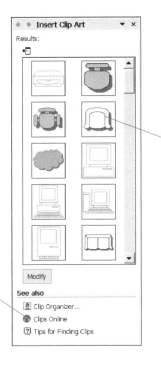

2 Drag an AutoShape into
your publication.

*For access to
more design
elements on
the web, click
Clips Online
and follow the on-screen
instructions.*

Changing the border

When you first draw a shape, Publisher applies a default border of a 0.75 pt plain black line. However, you can change the border style, thickness and colour, or even remove the border entirely. If you've drawn a box, you can even apply a fancy border using the Line/Border Style button on the Formatting toolbar. Follow the steps below to change the border of a shape:

1 Select the shape you want to border.

2 Click the Line/Border Style button on the Formatting toolbar:

Select No Line to remove a border.

No Line
¼ pt
½ pt
¾ pt
1 pt
1½ pt
2¼ pt
3 pt
4½ pt
6 pt
3 pt
4½ pt
4½ pt
6 pt
More Lines...

3 Select a border.

If your shape is a rectangle or box, you can replace a plain border with a fancy border. First click the shape to select it. Next, click the Line/Border Style button, followed by the More Lines command. Click the Colors and Lines tab, then the BorderArt button. Choose your desired border settings and click OK twice.

The result of applying a 6 pt border to clip art

Changing the fill colour

Publisher is rich in options which enable you to apply a different fill to a shape. Publisher gives every shape you draw a default fill colour and pattern. You can change colours, choose from a variety of patterns, or change both the colour and the pattern. To change the fill colour, perform the following steps:

1 Select the shape whose fill you want to change.

You can increase the number of colours in the Colour Palette:

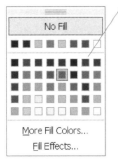

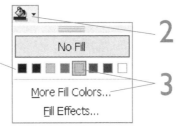

2 Click the Fill Color button arrow on the Formatting toolbar.

3 Click a colour. But if you can't see the desired colour, click More Fill Colors and follow step 4.

(When you do this, the colours you add are not part of any colour scheme. This is useful if you want to copy-and-paste objects between publications with differing schemes.)

In the Tools menu, select Options. Activate the General tab and tick Show basic colors in color palette. Click OK.

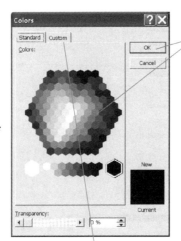

4 Click your desired colour, then OK. If you can't see the colour you want, perform steps 5–6.

6 Click an area of the colour chart or enter values in the edit boxes.

5 Define your own custom colour: click the Custom tab.

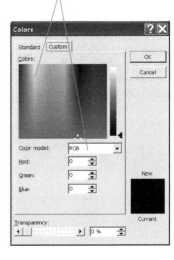

If you apply a fill and it doesn't work, make sure the object isn't obscured by an opaque text frame. If it is, select the frame and press Ctrl+T.

Changing the fill pattern

If you plan to use graduated fills in your publication, it's a good idea to make some test prints as soon as possible. Some printers can't handle some graduated fills and patterns easily, and therefore may substitute a chosen colour with a solid colour, or even black.

Fill patterns in Publisher can provide a stunning and powerful focus to an object. You can apply tints/shades, patterns and gradient fills. To change a shape's fill pattern, perform the following steps:

1 Select the shape whose pattern you want to change.

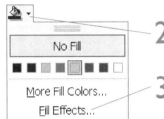

2 Click the Fill Color button arrow on the Formatting toolbar.

3 Click Fill Effects.

You can apply tints to objects. Tints are colours mixed with white. For example, a 30% tint has 3 parts of the colour and 7 parts white.

Simply activate the Tints tab and complete the dialog.

4 Select the relevant tab.

5 (Optional) Click a base colour and a second colour.

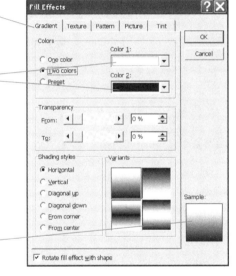

6 Click OK to apply your changes.

Publisher 2002 provides a sample of your choice here.

If you plan to print your publication commercially, avoid using patterns: they can work out more expensive.

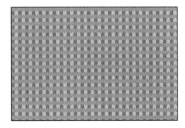

Before

After applying a 2-colour pattern

Making shapes 3D

Adding a sense of perspective to shapes can vividly enhance publications. To do this, perform the following steps:

You can make simpler AutoShapes 3D – see page 50.

You can only make Publisher shapes 3D, not inserted clip art.

1 Select the shape you want to make 3D.

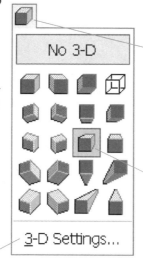

2 Click the 3-D Style button on the Formatting toolbar.

3 Click a 3D effect.

Click 3-D Settings for access to the 3-D Settings toolbar. You can use its buttons to:

- *turn 3D on/off*
- *tilt the 3D effect*
- *increase the 3D depth/ direction*
- *specify the light intensity/ direction*
- *specify the surface type*

A simple filled rectangle

After applying 3-D Style 17

Working with words

Your choice and use of words can shape the mood and tone of a publication, can persuade and entertain, and can ultimately hold or lose your readers' attention. In this chapter, we explore how to insert and manipulate text in a publication and how to change the look of text to create the finish you want.

Covers

Chapter Five

Importing text files

If you're working with multi-page documents containing mostly text, you may decide the job of preparing text for use in Publisher is easier if most of the typing is completed in your favourite word-processor. Publisher can accept text saved in a variety of common word-processor formats, including Microsoft Word, WordPerfect and Rich Text Format (RTF).

When you're compiling text from various sources, you may be dealing with text from several different formats. If your contributors cannot save their text files in a Publisher-compatible format, the safest option is to ask them to save in RTF format, which will keep most of the original formatting information. To import a text file into Publisher, carry out the steps below:

If you import or type more text than the target text frame can hold, Publisher stores the excess text in an invisible holding area. To ensure all text is made visible, first click the text frame to select it. Next, open the Format menu and choose AutoFit Text. Finally, from the fly-out menu choose either Best Fit or Shrink Text On Overflow.

1 If you're inserting text into a new location, draw a text frame with the Text Frame tool. If you're inserting text into an existing frame, click where you want the new text to start.

To turn off automatic copyfitting, follow the same procedure as above but choose the None command from the fly-out menu.

2 Open the Insert menu and click Text File.

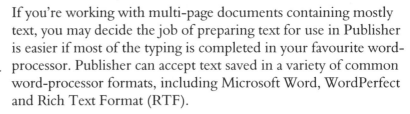

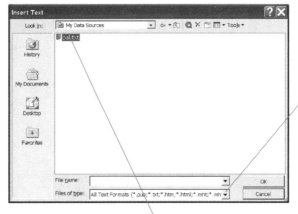

3 Optional – click here to see the range of file formats.

Re step 5 – if a further message launches, click Yes again to have Publisher create new text boxes/pages for you.

4 Find then double-click the desired text file.

5 If the text won't fit, click Yes in the message box to tell Publisher to automatically reflow excess text into new frames, or No to connect boxes yourself.

Entering text at the keyboard

If the amount of text is too large to fit in a text frame, you can apply three common solutions:

- *reflow the text to another frame (see page 27).*
- *enlarge an existing text frame, or;*
- *reduce the text size (see the HOT TIP on the facing page).*

There may be occasions when you've created a publication in Publisher, but you want to use some or all of the text in another non-Publisher-compatible document.

Publisher can save files in a range of different formats. So, if you're planning to use Publisher text elsewhere, and you know the application in which you expect to continue working on your Publisher-based text, try to save the file in a compatible format if possible. If you're not sure which application you'll be using, then save the file in RTF format.

To export a text file, choose Save As in the File menu. Name the file, then click in the Save as type: field and select an external format (e.g. Rich Text Format...). Choose a destination drive/folder and click Save.

The easiest way to create text in your documents is to draw a text block and simply begin typing (see the DON'T FORGET tip on page 25 for how to do this). Also, you can easily mix imported text with text you type: simply click where you want to start typing and begin. If the text appears too small because you're seeing your publication in full page view, with the text cursor flashing, press F9 to zoom in to actual size.

When you start typing, Publisher applies a default text size and formatting characteristics. You can change the text size, font, style and alignment later if you wish. Alternatively, you can apply these changes as soon as possible to get a better idea of how much space you'll need. Changing text formatting is examined later in this chapter.

If you're new to keyboard typing

When you begin typing, you don't need to press the Enter key at the end of every line: Publisher automatically wraps the text to the following line. When you want to start a new line or paragraph, simply press the Enter key. To indent a line, press the Tab key at the start of a new line. If you make a typing mistake, simply press the Backspace key to erase the last character typed.

Editing in Microsoft Word

If you have Microsoft Word version 6.0 or later installed on you PC or network, you can use Word to make your editing changes while working in your text frame in Publisher, and then return to your document to bring in the latest changes and updates, as follows:

1 Right-click inside a text frame.

2 In the floating menu, click Change Text, followed by Edit Story in Microsoft Word.

3 Edit your text in Word, then click Close & Return... in Word's File menu to return to your text frame.

Changing a font

Publisher comes with a wide range of different fonts and font styles. To recap, a font is a set of specific characters in a single typeface containing upper and lower case characters, punctuation marks and digits.

To change the current font, perform the following steps:

If the fonts in the Font box don't include what you want, you can install other fonts. See your Windows documentation for further information.

To quickly highlight all text in a text frame, click inside the desired text frame and press Ctrl+A. This is the keyboard shortcut for the Select All command in the Edit menu.

Different fonts of the same point size can take up varying amounts of space.

2 In the Font box on the Formatting toolbar, click the arrow to open the font list.

3 Click the desired font in the font list.

1 Select the text you want to change.

Using font schemes

To help you select and apply mutually compatible fonts, Publisher 2002 provides font schemes. Font schemes are collections of fonts which work well together and generally contain:

- a heading font

- a body text font

- a caption font

By applying a new font scheme, you can change the overall look of a publication in one easy step:

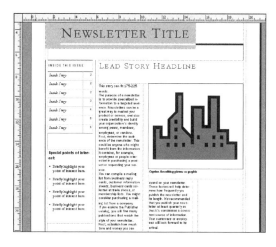

A standard newsletter publication

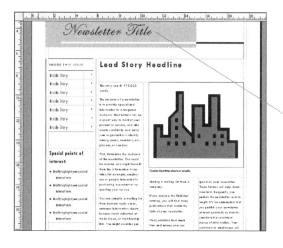

After applying the Monogram font scheme – notice particularly the new heading font

Applying a font scheme

1 In the Format menu, select Font Schemes.

Microsoft recommends the following font schemes for web pages:

- *Binary*
- *Foundation*
- *Virtual*

2 Select a font scheme.

You may need to manually verify the relaying operation.

3 Publisher applies the font scheme to the active publication, automatically relaying text frames to accommodate the changes in font and type size.

4 To customise the way Publisher applies font schemes, click the Font Scheme Options link at the base of the Task Pane. Complete the dialog which launches then click OK.

Changing text alignment

Justified text alignment applied to short text lines or lines containing large fonts can cause gap patterns or "rivers" of unsightly white space running down the page. To avoid this, use smaller font sizes and longer lines of text.

The way in which text is aligned within margins affects readability, and the impact that it makes. Publisher provides four ways to align text: flush left, flush right, centre and justified. By default, when you first create a text frame and begin typing, flush left alignment applies.

Considering text alignment options

Flush left alignment ensures that all lines in a text block align at the left margin, while flush right does the same at the right margin. Centred alignment centres each text line equally between the margins. Justified alignment spaces each text line equally between the margins.

Many people agree that text is easiest to read when aligned flush left (like this book). Flush right aligned text has a ragged left edge and consequently affects readability considerably. Not surprisingly, this is used sparingly.

To change the alignment of an entire block of text, select the entire block before choosing a text alignment button.

However, flush right alignment can provide a refreshing alternative when used with consideration. For example, letterheads containing names and addresses, company logos, pull quotes, and so on, can look distinctive and stylish when aligned at the right edge.

Centred alignment is ideal for headings, invitations and announcements; whereas justified alignment can provide a noticeable element of neatness, if the line width is wide and the font size reasonably small. To change text alignment, perform the following steps:

To align text vertically in its frame, first double-click the desired text frame. Then click the Text Box tab in the dialog which launches. Click in the Vertical Alignment box and select Top, Middle or Bottom (the default is Top). Click OK.

1 Click in the text frame containing the text you want to change (also see the HOT TIP in the margin).

2 Click one of the buttons on the Formatting toolbar shown below:

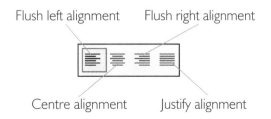

Flush left alignment   Flush right alignment

Centre alignment   Justify alignment

Changing the look of text

You can draw subtle or blatant attention to words or phrases by making the desired text **bold**, *italic*, or **both**. However, too much of either and the attention-gathering device ceases to work. Choose italics when you want to provide 'medium' emphasis, rather than underlining, to prevent the descenders of letters being 'cut off'.

You can also change emphasis by changing text colour; using more surrounding white space; or by the moderate use of small capitals.

To directly change the look of text, perform the steps below:

To quickly remove bold or italic formatting, highlight the desired text and click the appropriate button on the Formatting toolbar.

To change text to small capitals LIKE THIS, first select the text you want to change. Next, open the Format menu and click the Font command. In the dialog box, under the Effects category, tick Small caps. Finish by clicking OK.

1 Highlight the text you want to change.

2 To make text bold, click the Bold button.

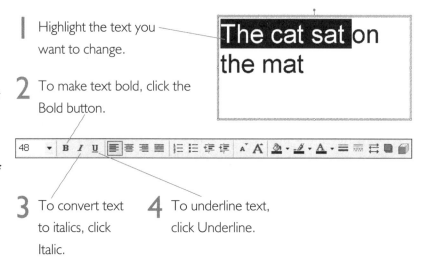

3 To convert text to italics, click Italic.

4 To underline text, click Underline.

5 (Optional) To change text colour, click the Font Color button arrow: Then click a new colour from the Colors palette.

Font style options include Regular, Italic, Bold, Bold/Italic, depending on the font.

To quickly remove all the formatting changes made to highlighted text, press the following keys: Ctrl+Spacebar.

Re step 5 – you can apply a variety of special effects to text. The example below shows Outline in action:

The cat sat on the mat

You can apply even more specialised effects to text, using the WordArt program that comes with Publisher. See chapter 6 for more information.

Changing multiple text properties quickly

To change several text format properties at the same time, first select the text. Then right-click it and choose Change Text, Font in the menu. Carry out the following steps, as appropriate:

1 Click here if you want to choose another font.

4 Click here to select an underline option.

3 Click here if you want to change the font style.

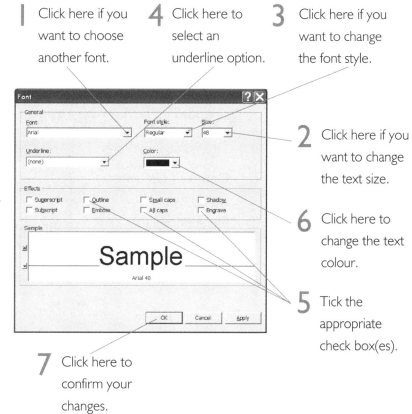

2 Click here if you want to change the text size.

6 Click here to change the text colour.

5 Tick the appropriate check box(es).

7 Click here to confirm your changes.

Making light text on a dark background

If you want to contrast light text on a dark background, first click in the desired text frame and press Ctrl+A.

On the Formatting toolbar, click the Font Color button, then click white from the Colors palette.

Next, also on the Formatting toolbar, click the Fill Color button and choose black from the palette. Lastly, click outside the selection.

Changing line spacing

Although Publisher automatically applies a default space between adjacent lines of text in each paragraph, you can easily change this value if you wish. However, if the adjustment is too much or too little for the font you're using, readability can become adversely affected.

To change line spacing, first click in the paragraph you want to change, or select all the text you want to affect. Then perform the steps below:

Publisher measures line spacing in inches, centimetres, points or picas. However, until you type in a different unit, Publisher uses 'sp' (current line space) units for values up to 4. If you type in a value higher than 4, Publisher, by default, uses points as the line spacing units.

1 Right-click the selected text, then choose Change Text, followed by Line Spacing from the floating menus.

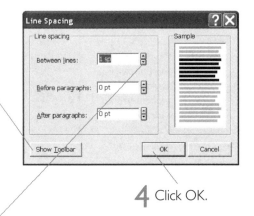

3 Optional – click here to display the Measurements toolbar (use it to change several text attributes at once).

4 Click OK.

If you want to change the line spacing units, type the appropriate abbreviation for the units you want to use, after entering the desired value in the Edit box:

- *'in' for inches*
- *'cm' for centimetres*
- *'pt' for points*
- *'pi' for picas*

2 Click the Up or Down arrow buttons to display the desired value in the Edit box. Alternatively, click in the Edit box and type the desired number value. By default, Publisher measures spacing between lines in 'sp' units. Each 'sp' (space) equates to the height of a line of the current text. Therefore, if you want to apply two line spaces between each line of text, enter 2 here.

Affecting a single line only

If you want the line spacing change to affect a single line only, press Enter before and after the desired line, to turn the line into a separate paragraph. Then apply the procedure described above.

Changing paragraph spacing

Publisher measures paragraph spacing in inches, centimetres, points or picas.

On the previous page, we examined how you can change the line-to-line spacing in a paragraph. In this section, we explore how you can change the amount of space between paragraphs.

You can increase or decrease the amount of space before and after a paragraph. To change the default paragraph-to-paragraph spacing, first click in the paragraph you want to affect, or select all the paragraphs you want to affect. Then perform the steps below:

If you want to change the paragraph spacing units, type the appropriate abbreviation for the units you want to use, after Entering the desired value in the Edit box:

- *'in' for inches*
- *'cm' for centimetres*
- *'pt' for points*
- *'pi' for picas*

1 Right-click the selected text, then choose Change Text, followed by Line Spacing from the floating menus.

2 In the Before Paragraphs box or the After Paragraphs box, click the Up or Down arrow buttons to display the desired value in the Edit box. Alternatively, click in the Edit box and type the desired number value. By default, Publisher measures spacing between paragraphs in 'pt' (point) units.

Re step 2 – to get an idea of size, there are 72 points to an inch (inches rather than centimetres are used here as points and picas are related to measurement in inches). Picas are also sometimes used; a pica is made up of 12 points.

Therefore, if you want to apply 8 points after each paragraph, you would enter 8 in the After Paragraphs edit box.

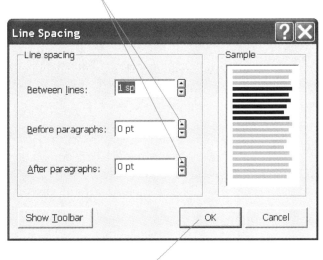

3 Click here.

Copying text

You can copy individual characters, words, sentences, paragraphs, entire text frames including text, and entire pages if desired. Also, if you have another Windows-based application open when Publisher is started, you should be able to copy text from that application to a document in Publisher.

Copying entire text frames

To copy an entire text frame, including its contents, to another location in the current Publisher document, perform the following steps:

Here's another way to quickly copy a text frame and its contents (or any other object). First, click inside the text frame to select it. Then, place the mouse pointer on the edge of the frame until you see the Move symbol. Hold down Ctrl then drag the text frame. When you release the mouse button, Publisher then creates an identical copy.

1 With the right mouse button, click in the text frame you want to copy.

2 From the floating menu, click Copy.

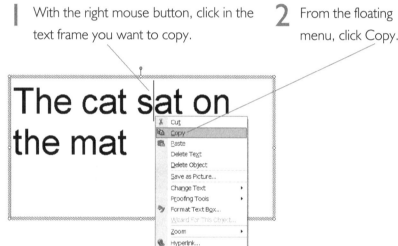

3 Move to where you want to place your copy. If you're copying to another page, move to the desired page.

4 Right-click any free space in the Workspace area.

5 From the floating menu, click the Paste command.

6 Drag the object to your desired location on the page.

You can then finely adjust the placing of the copied text frame.

The Copy and Paste commands are also available in the Edit menu. Also, other Windows applications may have Copy and Paste commands in their Edit menus, so you may be able to copy and paste information between Publisher and other applications.

Copying partial text

Sometimes, you may want to copy only part of the text in a frame. To do this, first select the text you want to copy. Then perform the following steps:

1 Right-click the highlighted text.

2 From the floating menu, click Copy.

You can copy and paste information between two Publisher documents. In the active document, copy the information you want. Then, open the destination document and paste the copied information where you want it.

3 Move to where you want to copy your text. If you're copying to another page, move to the desired page.

4 To finish, perform either step 5 or step 6. If you want to insert the copied text into an existing text frame, go to step 5. If you want to insert the copied text into a new text frame, go to step 6.

5 With the left mouse button, click where you want to insert your text. Then right-click inside the frame. Finally, from the floating menu, click the Paste command.

6 Right-click any blank area of the page (containing no objects). Then from the floating menu, click the Paste command.

Collect and Paste

If you want to copy-and-paste multiple items of text into a publication, you can now copy as many as 24 items. These are stored in a special version of the Windows Clipboard called the Office Clipboard, which in turn is located in the Task Pane. The Office Clipboard displays a handy visual representation of the data stored.

Using the Office Clipboard

Use standard procedures (see earlier) to copy multiple examples of text – after the second copy, the Clipboard appears in the Task Pane. Do the following:

To clear the contents of the Office Clipboard, click Clear All.

To call up the Office Clipboard at any time, pull down the Edit menu and click Office Clipboard.

You can also use the Office Clipboard to copy and paste other objects e.g. clip art.

Click the text you want to insert – it appears at the insertion point.

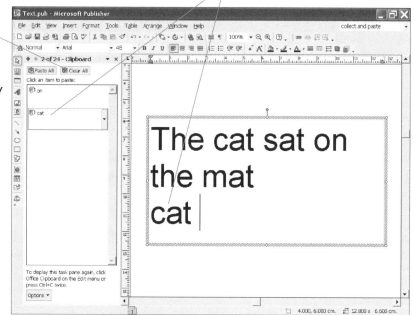

Moving text

Publisher provides several easy ways in which you can move text around a page; from page to page, and between Publisher documents. The method you use depends on several factors, such as whether you're moving an entire text frame or specific highlighted text. Remember also, you may be able to move text to a document in another application, if the destination application is compatible with Publisher.

To move an entire text frame within a document

1 Click inside the text frame you want to move.

2 Place the mouse pointer on the text frame border until the mouse pointer symbol changes to the Move symbol.

3 Hold down the left mouse button and drag the text frame to the desired location. If you want to move to another page, first place the text frame on the non-printing work area. Move to the desired page. Then drag the text frame onto the desired page.

To move specific text on the same page

1 Highlight the text you want to move. When you see the Drag symbol, drag to another location and release the mouse button.

DRAG

To move specific text within a document

1 Select the text you want to move.

2 Right-click the text to display the floating menu and choose Cut.

3 Move to where you want to place your cut text. If you're placing the text in an existing paragraph, click where you want to place it. To place your text in a new text frame, with the left mouse button click on a page outside of any objects. Next, right-click the page to display the floating menu. Finally, click the Paste command.

Deleting text

To delete a single character at a time, click where you want to delete. Then, each time you want to delete one character to the left of the insertion point, press the Backspace key.

You can delete specific text or an entire text frame easily in Publisher. However, sometimes you may want to delete text in frames but keep the frames in place. The following procedures describe your options when deleting text:

To delete some but not all text in a frame

1 Highlight the text you want to delete.

2 Press the Delete key.

To delete an entire text frame and the text within (method 1)

1 Right-click inside the text frame you want to delete.

2 From the floating menu, click the Delete Object command.

Each time you want to delete one character to the right of the insertion point, press the Delete key.

To delete an entire text frame and the text within (method 2)

1 Click inside the text frame you want to delete then press Ctrl+Shift+X.

If you accidentally delete text you want to keep, before performing any other action, click the Undo button on the Standard toolbar, or choose the Undo command in the Edit menu.

To delete all text in a chain of connected text frames without deleting the frames

1 Click inside one of the text frames in the connected sequence.

2 Press Ctrl+A (the shortcut to highlight all text in the chain).

3 Press the Delete key.

Finding specific text

You can use Publisher's Find command to quickly search for text containing specified characters in the selected text frame. If the text frame you're searching in is part of a connected chain, Publisher searches all the frames in the chain.

Before starting a search, make sure that all text has been flowed into text frames. Publisher can only locate fully flowed text. Any text which cannot be seen because it's located in the 'overflow' area, beyond the bottom of a text frame, will not be searched.

By default, Publisher flags all text containing the characters you specify. For example, if you Enter the characters 'ate', Publisher will flag 'create', 'date' and 'ate' if these words are present in the text. However, you can tell Publisher to find only exact specific text, if you wish, and limit the search criteria by specifying whether to flag only upper-case or lower-case characters.

Carry out the steps below to find the desired text:

1   Click the text or table frame in which you want to search.

2   Click the Find command in the Edit menu.

3   Type the characters you want to search for here.

Click here to limit the search to the exact characters in the 'Find what' box.

Click here to limit the search to text containing characters in the same case as the text in the 'Find what' box.

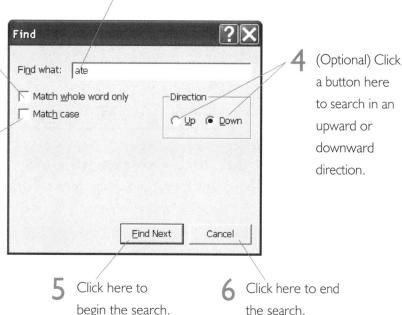

4   (Optional) Click a button here to search in an upward or downward direction.

5   Click here to begin the search.

6   Click here to end the search.

Replacing text with other text

To delete all instances of the text that you're searching for, simply leave the 'Replace with' edit box blank and click the Replace All button.

In addition to finding text, you can also tell Publisher to replace specific text with other text. If you're not sure of the exact spelling, you can still probably locate the desired text by using the 'wildcard' question mark symbol, as described in the search procedure shown below:

1 Click the frame in which you want to search and replace text.

If the selected frame is part of a series, Publisher will carry out the search and replace sequence in all frames in the chain.

2 Click Replace in the Edit menu.

3 Type the text you want to find here. Use a question mark for each character you're unsure of.

4 Here, type the text you want to replace the found text with.

Click here to limit the search to the exact characters in the 'Find what' box.

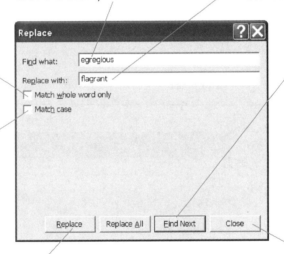

5 Click here to search for the desired text.

Click here to limit the search to text containing characters in the same case as the text in the 'Find what' box.

6 If Publisher finds the target text, click here to replace it and go to step 5 again. And so on. Alternatively, click Find Next to ignore the current find and continue the search.

7 Click here to end the search and replace sequence.

You can tell Publisher to replace all instances of the target text by clicking the Replace All button. However, remember you do lose control of the action, so be sure that this is what you want to do.

Advanced text features

Publisher contains some powerful yet easy-to-use text manipulation tools. In this chapter, we examine how to use these tools and how to create some common arrangements like bulleted/numbered lists, drop caps and indented text blocks. You'll also use WordArt to create dramatic text effects.

Covers

Chapter Six

Changing character spacing

To quickly highlight the entire text in a frame, press Ctrl+A.

Previously, we've examined how to change the spacing between lines of text and between paragraphs. Publisher also provides commands which enable you to alter the spacing between characters – also known as tracking.

This option can be useful if you want to improve the general look of text or to ensure specific text fits in the available space in a frame. For example, the look of headlines made up of larger font sizes can sometimes be improved by having their character spacing reduced.

When you change character spacing, Publisher makes a 'best guess'. Sometimes, characters may overlap. If this happens, click a looser spacing option in the Character Spacing dialog box.

To change character spacing in a specific paragraph, first highlight the desired paragraph. If you want to affect more than a single paragraph, highlight all the paragraphs you want to change. Then perform the following steps:

1 Open the Format menu and choose the Character Spacing command.

Tight spacing brings letters closer together; loose spacing moves letters further apart.

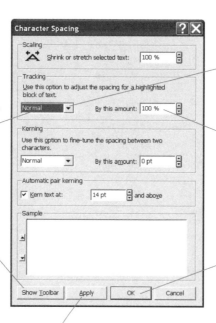

2 Click one of the preset options under the Tracking category (see the DON'T FORGET tip in the margin). Or choose the Custom option here and enter a new value in the By this amount box (range 0.1% to 600%).

Click here to show the Measurements toolbar, from which you can make multiple text formatting changes.

4 Click OK to make your changes.

3 (Optional) Click here to see (try out) your changes before you make them.

Changing character-pair kerning

To stretch or compress the width of characters, enter a value of between 0.1–600% under the Scaling option in the Character Spacing dialog box.

Kerning is the process of changing the spacing between certain pairs of characters that the human eye would otherwise perceive to be too close together or too far apart. The kerning values used vary from font to font.

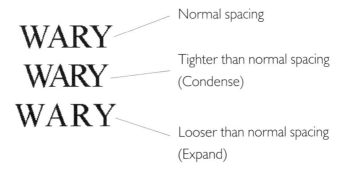

Normal spacing

Tighter than normal spacing (Condense)

Looser than normal spacing (Expand)

Here's the difference between tracking and kerning. Tracking adjusts the space between characters in a block of text; kerning adjusts the space between certain pairs of characters only.

To change the default kerning settings, first highlight the specific words or letters you want to change. Next, open the Format menu and click the Character Spacing command. Then, in the Character Spacing dialog box, carry out the following steps:

Publisher provides a visual representation of your changes as you make them. Also, you can click the Apply button to test out your proposed changes before confirming with the OK button.

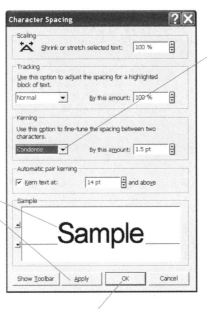

Under the Kerning category, click the option you want here. To increase the amount of space between characters, click Expand. To decrease the amount of space, click Condense.

2 Click OK to make your changes.

Working with symbols

You can change how a symbol appears by applying normal font formatting to the desired symbol.

Re step 3 – choose the Special Characters tab for easy access to typographical symbols e.g.:

— *Em dash*

– *En dash*

... *Ellipsis*

Often, you may want to include special symbols in your documents, like bullets (•), copyright (©) and trademark (™) (®) symbols, fractions, and so on. Publisher makes the job of including these in your documents easy. To place a symbol into your document, carry out the steps below:

1 In the text/table, click where you want to place the symbol.

2 Open the Insert menu and click the Symbol command.

3 Select the Symbols tab.

4 Click the symbol you want to use.

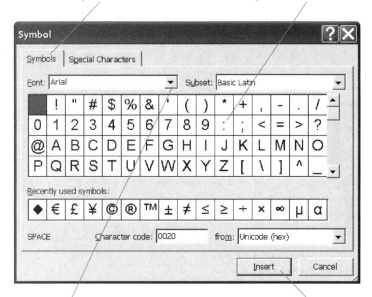

4 (Optional) If the desired symbol is not shown, click here to see other fonts installed on your PC.

5 Click Insert to place the selected symbol on the page or workspace.

Many useful graphic-based symbols are listed under the Wingdings category. You can see these by displaying Wingdings in the Font box in the dialog box.

Changing text frame margins

When you draw a text frame, Publisher applies default text margins within the frame. For most purposes, these default settings will probably be adequate. Sometimes however, you may want to change the margins. The following procedure shows you how to alter the size of the text frame margins:

You can enter a margin value for each side individually: Left, Right, Top or Bottom.

1 Click the text frame containing the margins you want to change.

2 On the Format menu, select Text Box.

3 Click the Text Box tab.

If you make the margins too wide, some of your text may seem to disappear. However, the excess text may only have flowed into the hidden overflow area under the text frame. Expand your text frame or create a new text frame and flow the excess text into it.

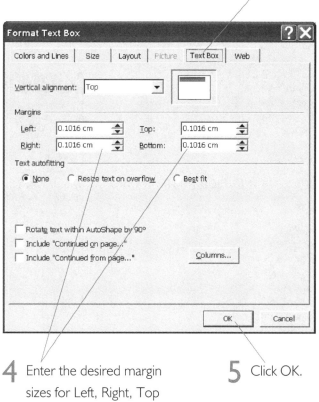

4 Enter the desired margin sizes for Left, Right, Top and Bottom margins.

5 Click OK.

Creating a bulleted list

To remove bullets from a list, first highlight the list. Next, right-click the highlighted list and choose Change Text followed by Indents and Lists. Under the Indents Settings category, choose Normal, then click OK.

When you want to present information in a clear but loose tabular form, often a bulleted or numbered list is an ideal answer. To create a 'standard' bulleted list:

1 Click where you want to start the list. (If you want to convert existing text to a bulleted list, highlight the text you want to convert first.) Then click the Bullets button: [icon] on the Formatting toolbar.

To create a customized bulleted list, select the text and:

1 From the Format menu, choose the Indents and Lists command.

If you can't see the symbol you want, click the New Bullet button and choose another font under the Font category.

To quickly create a bulleted list, first type an * (asterisk) followed by a space or tab and then type the text for your first line and press Enter. You can then continue to type the remaining entries for your list.

2 Click Bulleted list.

3 Click the bullet type you want.

4 (Optional) You can change the indent distance and alignment type here.

5 Click here.

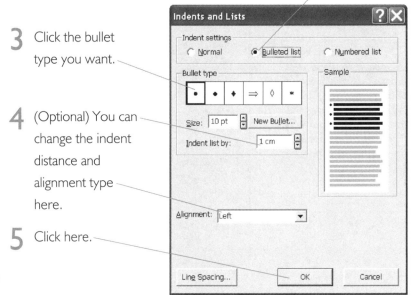

6 Type the text for your first line if you've not already done so. Then, each time you want to start a new line with a bullet, press Enter. To start a new line without inserting a bullet, press Shift+Enter. To end, press Enter twice.

Creating a numbered list

Numbered lists provide similar benefits to bulleted lists, except that a numbered list implies steps in a procedure or a hierarchy of priorities. To create a numbered list:

1 Click where you want to start the list. (If you want to convert existing text to a numbered list, highlight the text you want to convert first.) Then simply click the Numbering button: ▦ on the Formatting toolbar.

To remove numbering from a list, first highlight the list. Next, right-click the highlighted list and choose Change Text followed by Indents and Lists. Under the Indents Settings category, choose Normal, then click OK.

To create a customized numbered list, select the text and:

1 From the Format menu, choose the Indents and Lists command.

2 Click Numbered list.

3 Click the number format you want.

If you don't want the number sequence to start with '1', type a new value in the Start at: box.

4 (Optional) You can change the indent distance and alignment type here.

5 Click here.

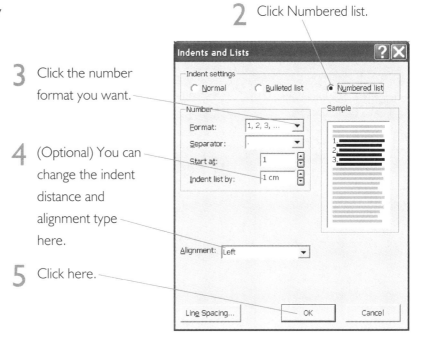

6 Type the text for your first line if you've not already done so. Then, each time you want to start a new numbered line, press Enter. To start a new line without inserting a number, press Shift+Enter. To end, press Enter twice.

Working with tab stops

If you prefer, you can insert, edit and delete tabs singly or in multiples, by using the Tabs command in the Format menu to display the Tabs dialog box.

Tab stops help you accurately place and align text vertically at specific positions in a text frame, and are particularly useful if you're dealing with tabular information. To indent text precisely and ensure that your printouts are accurate, it's important to use tab stops or indents rather than try to use the Spacebar. To set tab stops, first highlight the text you want to set up. Then perform the following steps:

The example uses the default left tab alignment. This means that Publisher aligns the tabs vertically at the left edge of the words.

1   On the ruler, click where you want tab stops to appear. Publisher indicates tabs with a marker.

To make tab marks (and other symbols e.g. spaces) visible in text, click this icon:

in the Formatting toolbar.

Space symbol

2   Click in the text where you want to place your tab, then press Tab. Repeat as necessary.

When you highlight text to change existing tabs, if you can't see the markers on the ruler, make sure that you've highlighted only the relevant text. If you highlight an area of text which does not have any tab formatting applied, Publisher does not display any tab markers on the ruler.

The Tab Alignment button has the following settings:

 Left tab alignment

 Right tab alignment

 Centre tab alignment

 Decimal point tab alignment

To change the status of tab stops and leaders, you must highlight the text which you want to affect, before choosing a command or starting a procedure.

Changing tab alignment

Publisher offers four tab alignment options:

- Left edge
- Right edge
- Centre
- Decimal point

You can change the alignment of highlighted text easily:

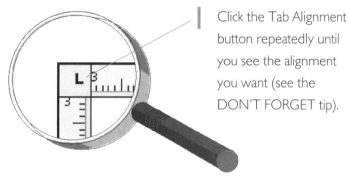

Click the Tab Alignment button repeatedly until you see the alignment you want (see the DON'T FORGET tip).

Moving and removing a tab stop

To move a tab stop marker on the ruler, simply drag the marker to a new position, or off the ruler to delete the tab.

Adding and deleting leaders to tab stops

To help guide the eye, you can add leaders – that is dots, dashes, or lines – to tab stops. Highlight the text you want to affect and double-click the desired tab stop marker on the ruler. In the Tabs dialog box, under the Leader category, click the leader you want. Then click OK. To delete leaders, highlight the text you want to affect, display the Tabs dialog box again, and click None in the Leaders category. Click OK to confirm your changes.

Deleting all tab stops at the same time

First, highlight the text you want to affect. Then, in the Tabs dialog box, click the Clear All button, followed by the OK button.

Indenting – an overview

You can achieve a similar effect by using tabs. However, indents are easier to apply (and amend subsequently).

Indents are a crucial component of publication layout. For instance, in most publication types, indenting the first line of paragraphs (i.e. moving it inwards away from the left page margin) makes the text much more legible.

Other document types can use the following:

*   hanging indents (where the first line is unaltered, while subsequent lines are indented)

*   full indents (where the entire paragraph is indented away from the left and/or the right margins)

Some of the potential indent combinations are shown in the illustration below:

To quickly adjust an indent, first highlight the text containing the indent you want to change. Then, on the ruler, place the mouse pointer on the desired indent marker and simply drag it to the new position.

> **This paragraph has a full left and right indent. It's best, however, not to overdo the extent of the indent: 0.35 inches is often more than adequate.**
>
> **This paragraph has a first-line indent. This type of indent is suitable for most document types. It's best, however, not to overdo the extent of the indent: 0.35 inches is often more than adequate.**
>
> **This paragraph has a hanging indent. It's best, however, not to overdo the extent of the indent: 0.35 inches is often more than adequate.**

Left & right indent

First-line indent

Hanging indent

Left margin (inserted for illustration purposes)

Right margin (inserted for illustration purposes)

Applying indents to paragraphs

Indenting text – the dialog route

Select the paragraph(s) you want to indent. Pull down the Format menu and click Indents and List. Follow steps 1–3 below.

| Click a preset indent option.

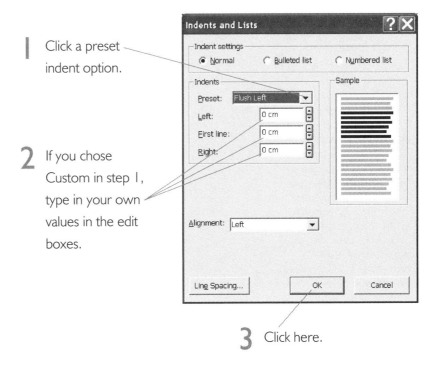

2 If you chose Custom in step 1, type in your own values in the edit boxes.

3 Click here.

If the Formatting toolbar isn't visible, pull down the View menu and click Toolbars, Formatting.

Indenting text – the toolbar route

First, select the relevant paragraph(s). Ensure the Formatting toolbar is visible. Then click one of these:

Using the Formatting toolbar route provides fewer indent options.

Increases the indent

Decreases the indent

Creating a text style

The easiest way to create a style is to:

A.   apply the appropriate formatting enhancements to specific text and then select it

B.   tell Publisher 2002 to save this formatting as a style

First, carry out A. above. Then pull down the Format menu and click Styles and Formatting. Now do the following:

Styles are named collections of associated formatting commands. The advantage of using styles is that you can apply more than one formatting enhancement to selected text in one go. Once a style is in place, you can change one or more elements of it and apply the amendments automatically throughout the whole of the active publication.

Click here.

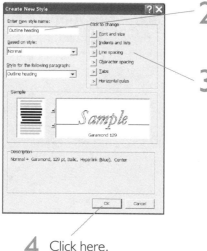

2   Name the style.

3   Optional – click any of these buttons (and complete the dialog) to adjust the style formatting.

4   Click here.

Applying a text style

You can delete user-created styles, if necessary. Carry out the following procedure.

Follow step 1. Right-click a style in the Task Pane. In the menu, select Delete. In the message which launches, click Yes.

First, select the text you want to apply the style to. Or, if you only want to apply it to a single paragraph, place the insertion point inside it. Pull down the Format menu and click Styles and Formatting. Now do the following:

2 Click a style.

You can rename user-created styles, if necessary. Carry out the following procedure.

Follow step 1. Right-click a style in the Task Pane. In the menu, select Rename. Complete the dialog.

Click here – in the list, select All Styles.

Shortcut for applying styles

Publisher 2002 makes it even easier to apply styles if you currently have the Formatting toolbar on-screen. (If you haven't, pull down the View menu and click Toolbars, Formatting.)

Select the text you want to apply the style to. Refer to the Formatting toolbar then do the following:

Click in the Style button; in the list, select a style.

This is an abbreviated view of the Formatting toolbar.

Amending a text style

The easiest way to modify an existing style is to:

A.   apply the appropriate formatting enhancements to specific text and then select it

B.   use the Styles and Formatting Task Pane to tell Publisher 2002 to assign the selected formatting to the associated style

First, carry out A. above. Choose Format, Styles and Formatting then do the following:

2   Right-click the relevant style – in the menu, select Update to match selection.

1   Click here – in the list, ensure All Styles is selected.

Using Personal Information Sets

When you create a new publication, Publisher will often give you the opportunity to amend/ enter personal information by launching the Personal Information dialog.

Personal information, whether for business or personal use, is often used repeatedly in publications. Publisher makes the job of handling repeated personal information easier by using Personal Information Sets.

A Personal Information Set contains basic essential information about you, your business or organisation. A group of components make up a Personal Information Set.

Each Personal Information Set contains the following eight components:

- Personal name
- Personal job title
- Name of organisation
- Address of organisation
- Organisation's tag line
- Telephone, fax and email numbers
- Organisation's logo
- Colour scheme

When you start a new publication, Publisher automatically selects the Primary Business Personal Information Set. However, you can choose which Set – if any – you want to use for the current publication using the Personal Information command in the Edit menu.

With a Personal Information Set, you need only enter this information once and from then on can choose to use it as it is, or modify it 'on the fly'.

Publisher makes available to you four Personal Information Sets. These are: Primary business (default); Secondary business; Other organisation; and Home/family.

Entering and updating personal information data

When Publisher 2002 is installed, it holds default personal information; you should replace this with your own data.

To enter the data that makes up your Personal Information components, or change the default Personal Information Set, perform the following steps:

Open the Edit menu and choose the Personal Information command.

To change information in a Personal Information Set, first make your changes as described here. Finally, save the publication.

When you save the publication, your Personal Information Set changes only apply to the current publication.

If you make a change to one instance of a Personal Information component in a publication, Publisher also changes all other instances of the same type of component to match.

Re step 1 – to add a logo component, select Logo in the submenu. Publisher inserts a logo. Click this icon:

In the Logo Designs Task Pane, select a logo design to apply it (see page 131 for more on this procedure).

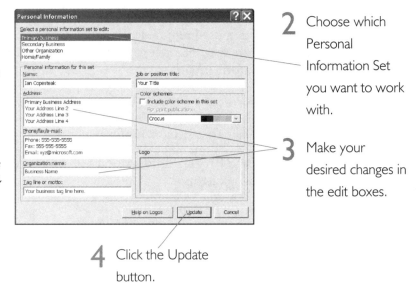

2 Choose which Personal Information Set you want to work with.

3 Make your desired changes in the edit boxes.

4 Click the Update button.

Adding a Personal Information component

1 Open the Insert menu, choose Personal Information followed by the specific Personal Information component you want.

2 Publisher inserts the chosen component object; you can then re-format, resize, reposition and even delete the component as desired, in the normal way. Shown is the Business Name component (but see the HOT TIP.)

WordArt

WordArt is one of Publisher's most powerful text design tools. Using the WordArt tool in the Objects toolbar, you can apply a range of special effects to text.

Using WordArt

Click the WordArt tool on the Objects toolbar:

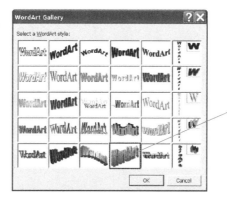

2 Double-click a design.

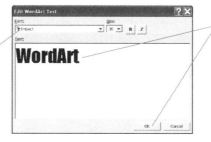

3 Type in the text you want to apply WordArt to and click OK.

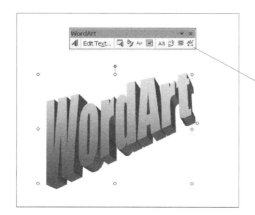

4 The WordArt text is inserted. Use the dedicated toolbar to apply various effects (e.g. apply text wrap or realign it).

Creating a drop cap

One of the most popular effects to include in a document is to add a fancy first letter – otherwise known as a drop cap – as shown below:

To create a drop first word, count the number of letters in the word. Next, perform steps 1–3 below. Click the Custom Drop Cap tab. In the Number Of letters box type the number of letters in the first word. Finally, click OK.

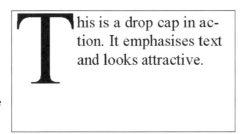

This is a drop cap in action. It emphasises text and looks attractive.

Many people prefer to apply this effect to the first letter in a frame of text. However, you can apply the same technique to an entire word if you wish. Carry out the steps below to create a drop cap:

1 Right-click the paragraph in which you want to add a drop cap.

2 Choose Change Text followed by the Drop Cap command.

To change or remove a fancy first letter, first click in the paragraph containing the letter. Next, click Drop Cap in the Format menu. To remove the letter, click the Remove button. To change the letter, click the Custom Drop Cap tab and make your changes. Finally, click OK.

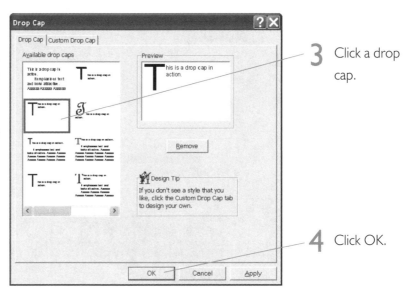

3 Click a drop cap.

4 Click OK.

Using mail merge

Publisher's mail merge feature shows how all mail merge tools should work. In this chapter, we describe how you can easily print customised address labels for mass mailing. You can also apply the same techniques and print hundreds of customised envelopes or other documents instead.

Covers

Chapter Seven

Setting up your data source

Publisher 2002 lets you set up a mail merge via an easy-to-use wizard.

Before you can tap the power of Publisher's mail merge feature, you'll need a mailing list of addresses (or other data source) which contains the individual records of information you want to apply to your publication.

Your data source can be created outside of Publisher, in a range of standard word-processor and database formats, like those from Microsoft Word, Access or Excel, dBASE and FoxPro. However, in this example, we'll create a list of addresses in Publisher itself, probably the most convenient option.

Creating an address list

| Pull down the Tools menu and select Mail Merge, Create Address List.

2 Enter information for the first address in the edit boxes.

After creating an address list, if you want to edit it click Tools, Mail Merge, Edit Address List. Then double-click on the list you want to edit.

3 Click here to save the first address then repeat step 2 for the second. And so on...

4 Click here then, in the Save As dialog which launches, name and save the list.

Using the Mail Merge Wizard

Once you have a suitable address list, you can launch the Wizard.

Step 1 – selecting an address list

1 Pull down the Tools menu and select Mail Merge, Mail Merge Wizard.

Re step 3 – select the list you created on the facing page. Or select another (e.g. a Word document containing address data as a table.)

Re step 5 – you can filter your data with even more precision. Click the arrow next to a column heading. In the menu, select (Advanced). Select the Filter Records tab. Click in the first box under the Field column and select the field that determines whether an entry will be included. Select a comparison (usually Equal to) in the field on the right; in the Compare to box, enter the value to be compared.

To apply further filters, select And or Or and repeat. Finally, click OK.

Re step 5 – for example, to sort by the address rather than the surname (the default), click:

After step 5, click OK.

2 Click here.

3 Click here. In the Select Data Source dialog, select the address list you want to work with then click Open.

6 Click here.

4 To remove an entry from the merge, untick it.

5 To sort data, click a column heading.

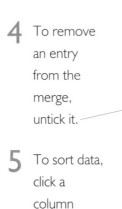

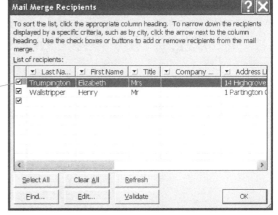

Step 2 – inserting data placeholders

7 Click a placeholder then (optionally) customise it. Click OK when finished.

For more placeholders, click More Items. In the Insert Merge Field dialog, click another placeholder and select Insert. Repeat for as many additional items as you need, then click Close.

In the example discussed in this chapter, the merge publication is a label. This was created by choosing Label in the New Publication Task Pane and clicking a design on the right of the screen (see step 1 on page 10 for more information). For illustration purposes, the default placeholders inserted by the Publication wizard were deleted.

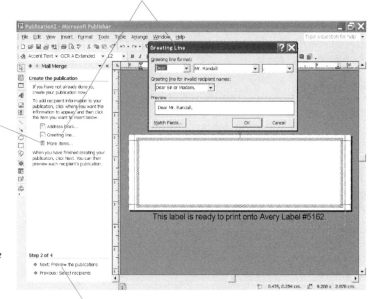

9 Repeat step 7 as often as required, then click here.

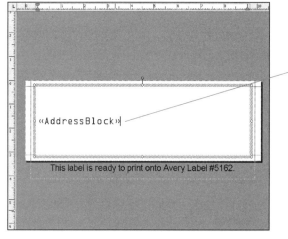

8 Publisher has inserted the placeholder(s)...

Step 3 – previewing the merge

I0 Publisher previews the first merge document.

You can change the size of the labels specified. Choose File, Page Setup. In the dialog, click the Layout tab then select the Label publication type. Select a new page size and click OK.

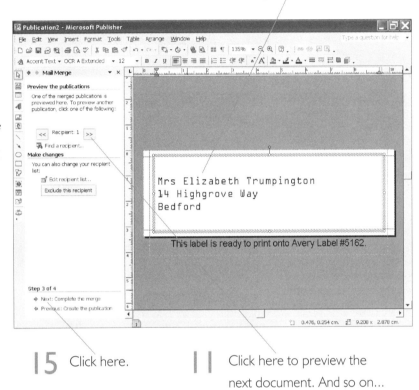

I5 Click here.

II Click here to preview the next document. And so on...

I2 Optionally – click Exclude this recipient to omit the current document from the merge.

I3 Optionally – to locate a recipient, click the Find a recipient... link.

I4 Enter the recipient's name and click Find Next.

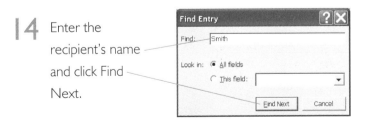

Step 4 – printing the merge

16 Ensure your printer is switched on and has enough paper.

To abort a mail merge (and sever the connection with your address list/data source), choose Tools, Mail Merge, Cancel Merge.

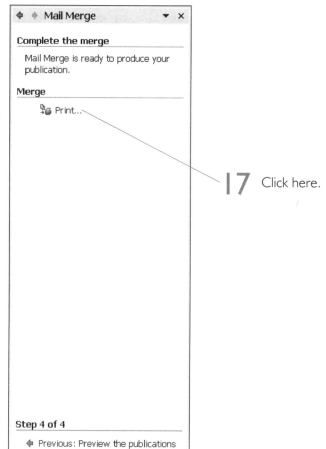

17 Click here.

Normally, the object of mail merges is to print the results. If you'd rather save the results to file, select Print to file in the Print dialog. Enter a file name in the Print to File dialog and click OK.

18 Complete the Print dialog and click OK to begin printing.

Working with tables

Tables can help show the big picture more quickly and bring some order and structure to a mass of information. This chapter explains how you can create and modify tables, including adding, deleting and changing rows and columns. We also look at how you can improve the appearance of a table by adding different types of borders, and pictures.

Covers

Chapter Eight

Creating a table

Tables are ideal if you want to organize words and numbers in a concise and compact form using rows and columns. Publisher makes the job of creating tables easy, and if you want to provide more sparkle to a table, you can apply various effects like shading, borders, add pictures, and so on, as shown in the example below:

As here, you can add pictures (and other objects) to your tables. See page 109 and chapter 9.

Raspberry sorbet	
Raspberries	500g
Kirsch	1 table spoon
Water	250 ml
Sugar syrup	
Sugar	200 g
water	250 ml

The information you put into a table can come from various sources. You can simply start typing in Publisher; copy from existing Publisher text or from another Windows-based application; or you can link or embed a table using OLE (examined on pages 43–44). Now let's look at how to create a table entirely from within Publisher: carry out the steps below and on the facing page:

1 On the Objects toolbar, click the Table Frame tool:

2 Position the mouse pointer where you want the upper-left corner of your table to appear. Press and hold down the left mouse button while you drag diagonally down to the right, until you see the table size and shape you want, then release the mouse button. It doesn't matter if the table is not exactly the correct size or shape: you can resize it later.

To vary the number of columns and/or rows, type in new values in the Number of rows or Number of columns fields.

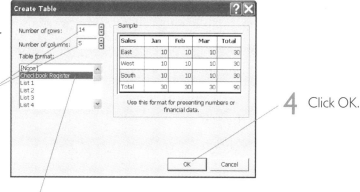

4 Click OK.

3 Click a table format from the list available.

Re step 5 – if your text fills the cell, Publisher automatically expands the cell to contain it.

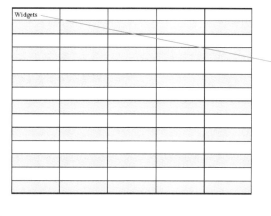

5 Publisher draws your table. Click where you want to start typing and type your entry for the current cell.

Table cell boundaries help provide a clear picture. If you can't see cell boundaries, click Boundaries and Guides in the View menu.

6 (Optional) In our example above, the first entry is a title. To arrange the title centrally across the top row of the table, first select the desired row by dragging the mouse across it. Then right-click over the cell and select Change Table followed by Merge Cells in the menu.

7 To move to the following cell, press Tab. To move to the previous cell, press Shift+Tab.

8 Complete your entries for the remaining cells in the table.

Moving around a table

On the previous page, you learnt how to move the insertion point to the following cell, or to the previous cell in a table.

Sometimes, Publisher provides alternative ways in which you can move through a table.

The following illustration summarises the options available to you for moving around a table.

Navigating through a table

Next Cell	Press Tab or the right cursor
Previous cell	Press Shift+Tab
Up one cell/line	Press the up arrow
Down one cell/line	Press the down arrow
Any cell	Click the cell
Any existing text	Click the text
Next character	Press the right cursor
Previous character	Press the left cursor
Next tab stop in a cell	Press Ctrl+Tab

Selecting in tables

When you want to change something in Publisher, you must select what you want to affect before choosing the relevant command. This is also true when working with tables, with some variations.

How to select any part of a table

Some text	Drag the mouse across the text
One word	Double-click it
All text in a cell	Click the cell then press Ctrl+A
Text in adjacent cells	Click where you want the selection to start. Hold down Shift and click where you want the selection to end
A specified cell	Drag the mouse across it
Any number of neighbouring cells	Drag the mouse across them
One row or column	See below
Multiple rows or columns	See below
Entire table	Click in one cell. Press Ctrl+A as often as required

Re step 1 – to select multiple columns or rows, just drag over them.

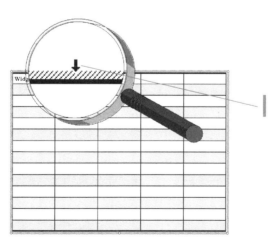

To select a whole row or column, move the mouse pointer over its edge. When it changes to a small arrow, click once.

Changing row and column size

Sometimes, as you add and modify cell contents in a table, rows and columns may need to be resized to display cell contents clearly and neatly.

Resizing a row or column

1   If the table is not already selected, click it.

2   Position the mouse pointer on the boundary of the row or column you want to change until you see the Adjust symbol appear:

3   With the appropriate Adjust symbol visible, hold down the left mouse button and drag the row or column boundary to display the new row height or column width, then release the mouse button.

Resizing an entire table

The task of resizing an entire table is made easier by the fact that Publisher considers a table to be an object. (In Chapters 2 and 3, we examined the properties of objects.)

Carry out the following steps (when you resize a table in this way, the proportions of all cells are affected to the same extent):

1   Click the table to select it.

2   Place the mouse pointer over one of the Selection handles until you see the Resize symbol.

3   Drag the mouse to display the table size you want.

4   Release the mouse button.

Adding rows and columns

Choose Table, Insert. In the submenu, select Columns to the Left, Columns to the Right, Rows Above or Rows Below.

After you've created your basic table, you may want to insert more rows or columns. You can do this using the Table menu, or by using the floating menu which Publisher displays when you right-click.

Inserting rows or columns

1 With the left mouse button, click in the row or column next to where you want to insert a new row or column.

2 With the mouse pointer placed on the table, right-click to display the floating menu.

To quickly add a row at the bottom of a table, click in the lower-most right cell in the table and press the Tab key.

3 Select Change Table, Insert.

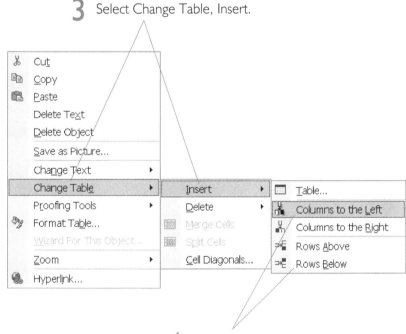

4 Select the appropriate option.

Moving and copying cell data

After developing a table, you may decide you want to move the contents of some cells, either to somewhere else within the same table, to another Publisher table, or even to another compatible Windows-based application. To move and copy information, Publisher provides the Cut, Copy and Paste commands in the Edit menu: commands which are also accessible by right-clicking.

Moving cell data

To quickly move a cell's text to another location, first highlight the cell containing the text you want to move. Next, place the mouse pointer over the highlighted cells until you see the Drag symbol. Hold down the left mouse button and drag the highlighted text to the new location. Finally, release the mouse button.

1 If you want to move or copy cell data to another table in another Publisher document, open the publication to which you want to move the cell data. This is the target document.

2 Back in the source document, highlight the table cells containing the information you want to move or copy.

3 Right-click the cells you want to move or copy.

4 On the floating menu, click the Cut command to move data or the Copy command to copy data.

Two successive copy operations invoke the Clipboard Task Pane – see

page 68.

5 In the destination table, if you want to replace existing cells, highlight the cells to which you want to move or copy data. But if you want to move or copy to new empty cells, click the cell in which you want the upper-left corner of the cut text to be placed.

6 Right-click – in the menu, select Paste.

Deleting rows and columns

To delete a row or column, carry out the steps below:

1 Highlight the row(s) or column(s) you want to delete (see step 1 on page 101).

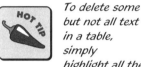 *To delete some but not all text in a table, simply highlight all the text you want to delete, then press the Delete key.*

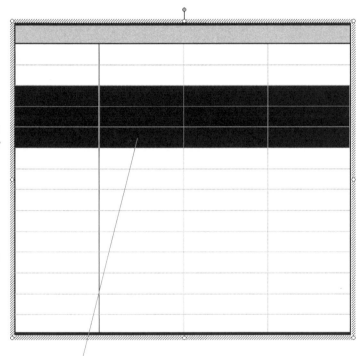

 To quickly delete an entire table, right-click the table's frame. From the floating menu, click the Delete Object command.

2 Right-click the highlighted row or column.

3 In the menu, select Change Table, Delete.

4 In the submenu, select Rows or Columns.

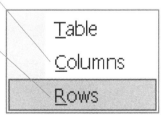

Changing how cell data looks

There are several ways in which you can enhance the appearance of a table and make it more attractive and clearer to see. You can use crisp, clear fonts and apply colours – if appropriate. Table titles and subheadings can be easily identified at a glance when they consist of light-coloured text on a dark background. Also, subtle shading helps provide a medium level of importance in a hierarchy of headings, as shown in the example below:

Population·growth·since·1900			
Year¤	Population¤	Year¤	Population¤
1900¤	96,936¤	1950¤	24,719,045¤
1910¤	367,924¤	1960¤	37,205,128¤
1920¤	1,267,490¤	1970¤	46,196,826¤
1930¤	5,829,045¤	1980¤	68,668,295¤
1940¤	17,492,594¤	1990¤	79,583,999¤

Sometimes shading can interfere with the clarity of a table.

Therefore, if using lighter, smaller sized fonts, you may consider shading is not a worthwhile option.

Applying shading to a table

1 Highlight all the cells to which you want to apply shading.

2 On the Formatting toolbar, click the Fill Color button arrow:

3 Click Fill Effects.

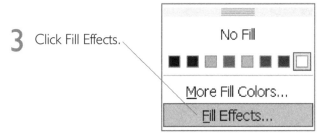

4 Use the Fill Effects dialog box to apply the shading options you want (see page 53 for more information) then click OK.

Changing the colour of objects

You can easily change the colour of cells, rows and columns, cell text and table borders, in addition to changing or adding shading and patterns to cells.

Changing text colour

1 Select the cells you want to recolour.

2 On the Formatting toolbar, click the Font Color button arrow:

3 Select a colour. Or click More Colors and select one in the Colors dialog.

Changing the cell colour

1 Select the cells, rows or columns you want to recolour.

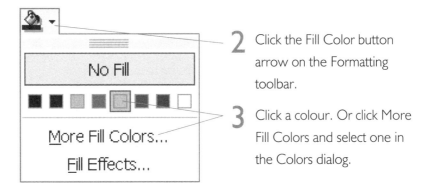

2 Click the Fill Color button arrow on the Formatting toolbar.

3 Click a colour. Or click More Fill Colors and select one in the Colors dialog.

Merging and unmerging cells

As you develop a table, sometimes you may want to merge several cells in a specific row. For example, we often merge cells when inserting a table title or subtitle as shown in the illustrations on these pages. Cells that you choose to merge must all be in the same row.

Merging cells

1 If the table is not already selected, click it.

2 Highlight the cells you want to merge then right-click them.

3 In the menu, click Change Table, Merge Cells.

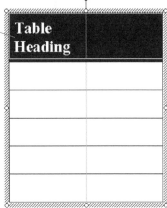

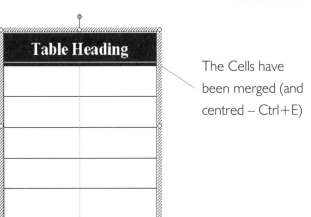

The Cells have been merged (and centred – Ctrl+E)

If you change your mind, you can quickly unmerge cells by first performing steps 1–2 above. Then click Change Table, Split Cells in the contextual menu.

Adding an object to a table

To provide a focal point or to add greater visual impact to a table, you can add objects like pictures. However, if you add objects to a table in this way, they do not become part of the table in the same way as a table cell. Rather, a picture is overlaid onto a cell or several cells as shown in the illustration below.

Including a picture or other object in a table

1 On the Objects toolbar, click the Picture Frame tool:

2 Draw a frame on top of the table cell or cells which you want to contain your picture.

3 Use the Insert Picture dialog to locate and insert the relevant picture.

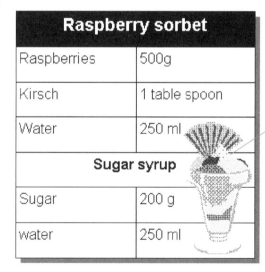

Raspberry sorbet	
Raspberries	500g
Kirsch	1 table spoon
Water	250 ml
Sugar syrup	
Sugar	200 g
water	250 ml

Here, an appropriately chosen picture is placed to enhance the table, creating a compelling presentation

You may need to resize and move your object to display it in the desired position. Remember, you can use Publisher's layout guides, zoom commands and the Shift key to help accurately resize and align an object.

Applying cell and table borders

Normally, when you create a table, Publisher inserts cell boundaries around each cell. As explained at the beginning of this chapter, these cell boundaries may be visible. If they're hidden, you can make them visible by clicking the Boundaries and Guides command in the View menu.

However, cell boundary lines don't print out: they simply show where one cell ends and another begins. To apply a cell border to each cell, carry out the following steps:

1 Highlight the entire table (or only the cells to which you want to apply grid lines) then right-click them.

2 In the menu, select Format Table.

3 Ensure this tab is active.

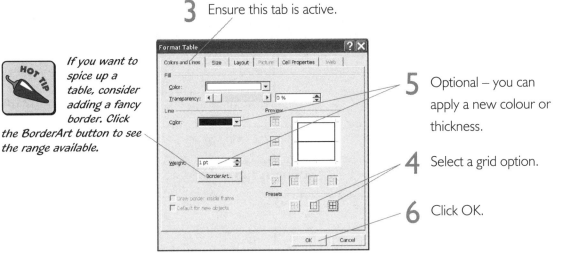

If you want to spice up a table, consider adding a fancy border. Click the BorderArt button to see the range available.

5 Optional – you can apply a new colour or thickness.

4 Select a grid option.

6 Click OK.

A shortcut

You can use a shortcut to border cells. Select the relevant cell(s). On the Formatting toolbar, click the Line/Border Style button:

In the drop-down menu, select a preset border.

Working with pictures

Sometimes pictures can tell us most of what we need to know about a topic at a glance. In this chapter, we explore how to insert and manipulate pictures in a publication. You'll also learn how to apply clip art pictures from the Clip Organizer to further enhance your publications, and you'll get to know Organizer's features in some detail.

Covers

Chapter Nine

Inserting clip art

Re step 1 – enter no keywords to view all clips.

Inserting clip art via the Clip Art Task Pane

Pull down the Insert menu and click Picture, Clip Art. Now carry out the following steps:

1 Enter one or more keywords.

Clips have associated keywords. You can use these to locate clips.

3 Click Search.

You can add new clips to collections (or add new keywords to existing clips) in the Clip Organizer.

Click here to launch it: then see later in this chapter.

2 Optional – click here and make the appropriate choices.

To conduct another search, click the Modify button then repeat steps 1-3.

4 Click an icon to insert the clip.

For access to more clips, click Clips Online and follow the on-screen instructions.

Working with the Clip Organizer

By default, the Clip Organizer comes with numerous pre-defined collections e.g.

- Business

- Character Collections

- Communication

- Fantasy

- People

Launching the Clip Organizer

If the Clip Organizer isn't already open, pull down the Insert menu and do the following:

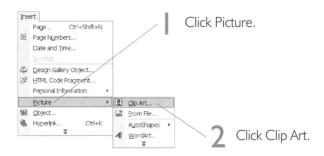

I Click Picture.

2 Click Clip Art.

3 Click Clip Organizer.

Inserting clips via the Organizer

You can access clips on the web by clicking the following Organizer toolbar button:

Microsoft's Design Gallery Live site launches:

Use this to locate and download extra clips.

To remove a clip from the Organizer (but not your hard disk), right-click it. In the menu, click Delete from Clip Organizer. In the message which launches, click OK.

To add an AutoShape or WordArt object to the Organizer, select it. Press Ctrl+C. In the Organizer, go to the collection folder you want to add it to (but not those in Office Collections) and press Shift+Insert – a copy of the object is inserted as a clip.

You can use the Clip Organizer to insert clip art into your publications. This is a useful technique.

1 If the Clip Organizer isn't currently open, follow steps 1-3 on page 113.

3 Drag a clip onto your publication.

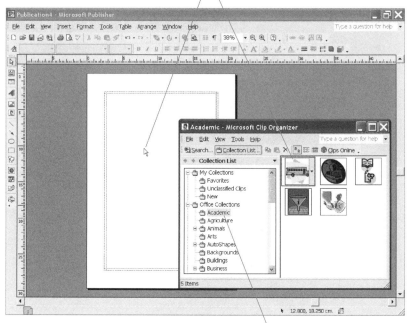

2 Click a collection.

4 Resize and/or reposition the picture in the usual way.

Creating new collections

To have Organizer search for media files and organize them into collections for you (see My Collections here), choose File, Add Clips to Organizer, Automatically. In the dialog, click OK.

To create a new collection, do the following:

1 If the Clip Organizer isn't currently open, follow steps 1-3 on page 113.

2 Click Collection List, then select My Collections.

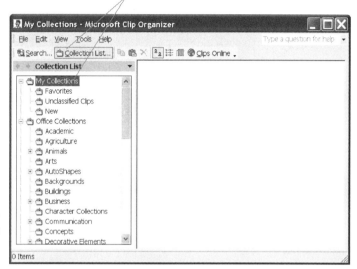

To manually add a clip to the Organizer, pull down the File menu and click Add Clips to Organizer, On My Own. Use the Add Clips to Organizer dialog to locate and select the clip you want to add (first ensure the Files of type: field shows the correct format e.g. Pictures). Now click Add To. In the Import to Collection dialog, select a host collection. Click OK.

Finally, back in the Add Clips to Organizer dialog, click Add.

3 Pull down the File menu and click New Collection.

5 Name the collection.

You can only create a new collection from within My Collections.

4 Select a destination folder.

6 Click here.

Renaming collections

If the Clip Organizer isn't currently open, follow steps 1-3 on page 113.

When Clip Organizer creates collections automatically, their names are based on the host folders. You can easily rename these...

You can't rename the collections supplied with Clip Organizer.

To delete a collection, follow steps 1– 2. In step 3, select Delete... In the message, click Yes.

When you delete a collection (see the above tip), the associated clips are not deleted.

To preview a clip and view associated information, right-click it in the Organizer (or after a search in the Insert Clip Art Task Pane) and select Preview/Properties. Press Esc when you're through.

2 Right-click a folder under My Collections.

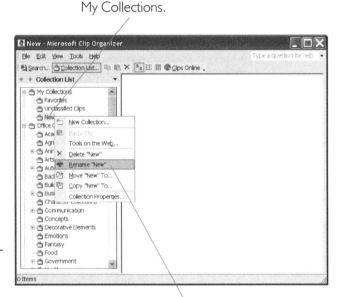

3 Click Rename...

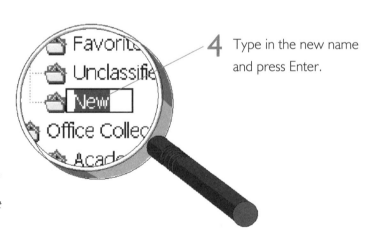

4 Type in the new name and press Enter.

Using keywords

When clips are added to the Clip Organizer (either manually or automatically – see the HOT TIPs on page 115), certain keywords are routinely added to them. These are based on the name or suffix, but you may want to add your own keywords (so you can locate the clips more easily later).

Clips in the Clip Organizer can (and do) have keywords associated with them. This means, for instance, that if you want to find a specific picture you can run a keyword search – see page 118. You can add additional keywords to any clip.

Adding keywords to a clip

Do the following:

1 If the Clip Organizer isn't currently open, follow steps 1-3 on page 113.

To find related clips, right-click a clip in the Organizer (or after a search in the Insert Clip Art Task Pane) and select Find Similar Style.

2 Select a collection.

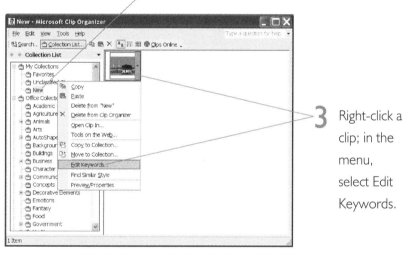

3 Right-click a clip; in the menu, select Edit Keywords.

You can use a shortcut to email a clip to someone. Choose File, Send to Mail Recipient (as Attachment). Complete the New Message dialog and click Send.

4 Enter a new keyword and click Add.

To change an existing keyword, select it in the Keywords for current clip field in the Keywords dialog. Amend the keyword in the Keyword box and click Modify.
  To delete a keyword, highlight it in the Keywords for current clip field and click Delete.

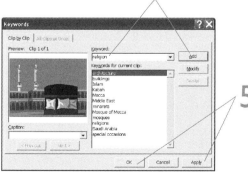

5 Click OK or Apply.

Searching for keywords

You can also run a search from the Insert Clip Art Task Pane. Follow steps 3-4 (and see the tip below).

To search for clips by one or more keywords, do the following:

1 If the Clip Organizer isn't open, follow steps 1-3 on page 113.

 2 Click Search.

3 Enter keyword(s) – see the DON'T FORGET tips on the facing page.

If you want to customise the search, do one or both of the following:

- *click here; in the list, select a collection to search in (e.g. Office Collections, or specify an individual collection)*

- *click here; in the list, specify a search format (e.g. Clip Art or Photographs)*

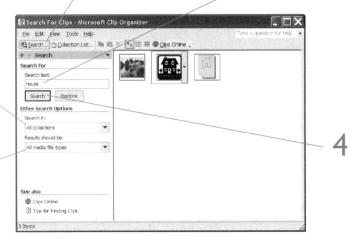

4 Click Search.

Moving the mouse pointer over a clip produces a box listing the first few associated keywords:

The end result:

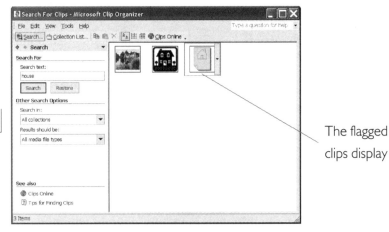

The flagged clips display

If your web connection is live when you run a search, Publisher automatically searches content on Microsoft's Design Gallery Live site.

Inserting pictures – an overview

Re step 3 on the facing page – you can also search for filenames.

Additionally, you can use standard wildcards – for example, to find all BMP files, type in:

*.bmp

Alternatively, to locate a clip called 'plane1.tif' (but not 'plane12.tif'), search for:

plane?.tif

(The last method would also find 'plane5.tif' and 'plane8.tif'.)

Re step 3 on the facing page – the table below illustrates the syntax you can use:

To find the unconnected keywords *red* and *bus*	Type in: red bus
To find the phrase *red bus*	Type in: "red bus"
To find *red* or *bus*	Type in: red, bus

Pictures Publisher 2002 can import into publications fall into two overall categories:

- bitmap images
- vector images

The following are brief details of each (note particularly that there is a certain level of crossover between the two formats):

Bitmap images

Bitmaps consist of pixels (dots) arranged in such a way that they form a graphic image. Because of the very nature of bitmaps, the question of 'resolution' – the sharpness of an image expressed in dpi (dots per inch) – is very important. Bitmaps look best if they're displayed at their correct resolution. You should bear this in mind if you're exporting files from other programs for inclusion in Publisher 2002 publications.

Publisher 2002 imports (i.e. translates into its own format) a variety of third-party bitmap formats.

Vector images

Publisher 2002 will also import vector graphics files in formats native to other programs. Vector images consist of, and are defined by, algebraic equations. One practical result of this is that they can be rescaled without any loss of definition. Another corollary is that they're less complex than bitmaps: they contain less detail.

Vector files can also include bitmap information. For example, PostScript files often have an illustrative header (used for preview purposes) which is generally a low-resolution bitmap. This header is very often considerably inferior in quality when compared to the underlying picture.

Inserting pictures

Re steps 1–2 – choose Picture, From Scanner or Camera instead to insert input from a scanner or camera. Now select the relevant device and follow the on-screen instructions.

To border clip art, select it. Click the following button in the Picture toolbar:

In the drop-down list, click a preset border option.

You can also use the Picture Frame tool in the Objects toolbar to insert pictures. See page 109.

Go to the publication into which you want the picture added. Pull down the Insert menu and do the following:

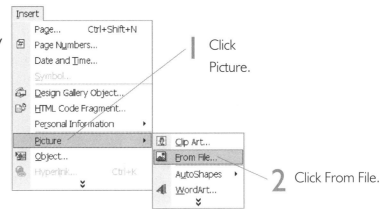

1 Click Picture.

2 Click From File.

4 Click here. In the drop-down list, click the drive/folder that hosts the picture.

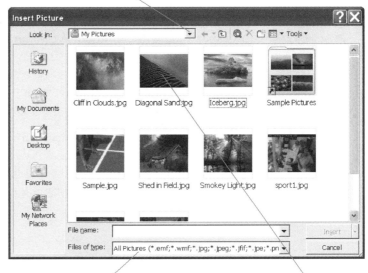

3 Make sure All Pictures... is showing. If it isn't, click the arrow and select it from the drop-down list.

5 Double-click a picture file.

Working with clip art/pictures

You can perform the following actions on clip art/pictures:

To recolour clip art, select it. Click the following button in the Picture toolbar:

In the menu, click Grayscale, Black & White or Washout (creates a watermark effect).

- resizing/cropping

- recolouring (to a limited extent)

- bordering (see the facing page)

Resizing clip art/pictures

Select the clip art/picture. Now do the following:

Drag any handle inwards or outwards

Re step 2 – the following table displays some tips to help you crop more effectively:

To crop from two sides at once	Hold down Ctrl as you drag in one centre handle
To crop from all sides at once	As above, but drag in a corner handle

Cropping clip art/pictures

Select the image. Refer to the Picture toolbar (View, Toolbars, Picture) and do the following:

Click here.

2 Click the picture – the handles are angled. Move the mouse pointer over a handle until if forms a smaller version of it and drag in.

To undo a crop, press Ctrl+Z. You can also use another method. Right-click the image and choose Format Picture. In the Format Picture dialog, select the Picture tab then Reset. Click OK.

Before…

After

Changing the screen redraw speed

The size and complexity of a picture (especially photographic images), and the speed with which your computer processes complex images, affect how quickly your PC draws an image on the screen. If you find images are taking too long to redraw when you zoom or move from page to page, you can reduce the resolution or even hide the images entirely, leaving picture placeholders where your pictures would normally appear while working on the general layout of your document.

If you reduce the resolution of your picture display, or hide a picture as described below, when you print, your printer can still print pictures using its full resolution.

If you've reduced the picture display resolution, but later want to re-display it at full resolution, first click Pictures in the View menu. Next, click Detailed display followed by OK.

Changing your picture display resolution

First click Pictures in the View menu. Then carry out the steps below:

I To speed up the picture redraw speed of Publisher-based images, click Fast resize and zoom.

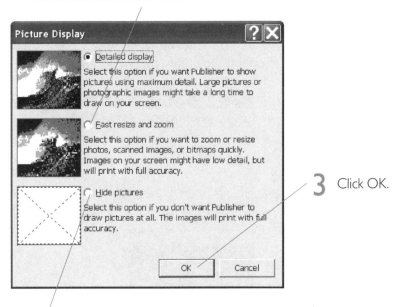

3 Click OK.

2 Alternatively, to have Publisher hide pictures and replace each one with a boxed X as a placement reference, click Hide pictures.

Considering page design

How your pages look makes a difference. This chapter focuses on how Publisher can help you achieve the effect you want. We explore the Design Gallery and take a closer look at the use of BorderArt. We also delve into some of the most eye-catching design aspects – logos, mastheads, and the techniques of flowing text around a picture.

Covers

Chapter Ten

Opening the Design Gallery

The Design Gallery is an excellent collection of predesigned objects which you can include in your publications. The text and graphic objects typically include: headline and masthead designs, pull-quotes, forms, table of contents designs, logos, advertisements and calendars.

The Design Gallery provides an excellent platform on which you can combine your own ideas and try different combinations to see which produces the results you're looking for.

Many of the objects are designed to match the styles used in Publisher's PageWizards. For example, if you used the Brochure PageWizard (see chapter 1), the Design Gallery can offer alternatives by matching components to include with or instead of objects already placed.

You can also store design elements which you create in the Design Gallery, allowing you to access them easily again and again. Publisher also makes the job of finding your design elements easy by grouping related objects into categories. If you can't find the right category in which to store an object, simply create a new category to suit your needs.

To open the Design Gallery, click the Design Gallery Object button on the Objects toolbar. The Gallery launches:

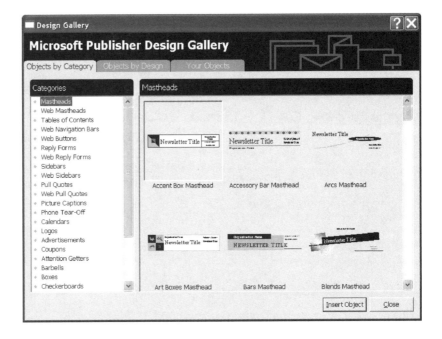

Choosing a Design Gallery object

Sometimes more designs are available than can be seen. Use the scroll buttons to see the hidden designs if they're available.

To add an object from the Design Gallery to your publication, first click the Design Gallery Object button on the Objects toolbar, then carry out the steps below:

| Click the tab you want: you can view objects by Category, by Design, or Your own Objects (examined later).

3 Click the object you want.

Double-click an object's icon to quickly place the object on the page.

To import an object into Design Gallery, see page 127.

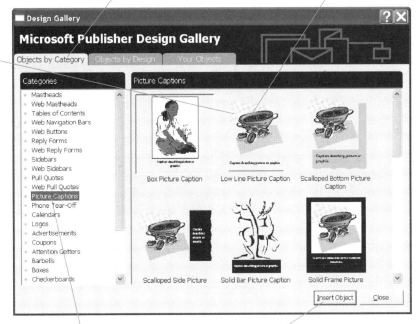

2 Click the Category you want.

4 Click the Insert Object button.

5 Publisher places your chosen object on the page.

Changing a Design Gallery object

After you've placed a Design Gallery object, you can still experiment with different designs. Here's how:

On the object, click the 'Wizard: Click to start' button.

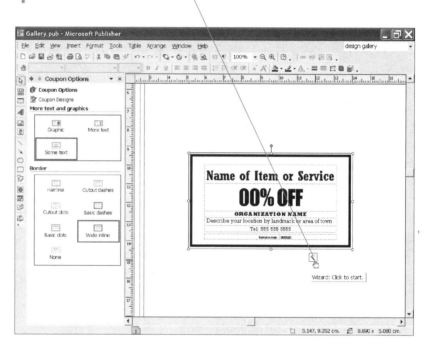

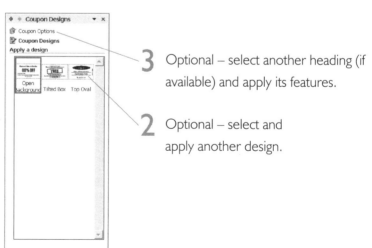

3 Optional – select another heading (if available) and apply its features.

2 Optional – select and apply another design.

When you've finished, simply click any empty space on the page or workspace.

Adding objects to the Gallery

With every new publication, Publisher creates an empty design set. You can add design elements to the current document design set, to the design sets that come with Publisher, or to objects from other compatible documents. On this page, we're going to add objects to the current document design set. To do this, perform the steps below:

1 Click the design element you want to add to the current design set.

Objects you add to the Gallery are not available to any other Publisher publications.

2 Click the Add Selection To Design Gallery command on the Insert menu.

3 Type a name for the object you're adding.

4 Click the Category you want from the drop-down list or type a new Category name here.

5 Click OK to add the object to the desired Category.

6 Save the current publication. Any objects you add to the Design Gallery for this publication are then saved as part of the publication's design set.

Deleting Design Gallery objects

You can delete objects that you store in the Design Gallery listed under the Your Objects tab, for the publication you're currently working on. However, you can't delete any of Publisher's own Design Gallery objects – that is, those available from the Objects by Category and Objects by Design tabs.

Deleting a Design Gallery object

After you've deleted a Design Gallery object, it's not really deleted until you save the current publication.

If you delete an object by mistake, simply close the current publication without saving it, then reopen the publication – the 'deleted' object will still be available.

Publisher only records the changes you've made to the Design Gallery when you save the current publication. Therefore, it's a good idea to save immediately after making any important changes here.

1 Click the Design Gallery Object button on the Objects toolbar:

3 Click the Category containing the object you want to delete.

2 Click here to display your objects.

4 Right-click the object; in the menu, select Delete This Object.

5 In the message which appears, click Yes to confirm you want to delete the object.

Creating Design Gallery categories

You can create a new category and add it to the design set of the current publication.

Creating a new category

1 Click the Design Gallery Object button on the Objects toolbar:

2 Click here to display your objects.

Categories you add to the Gallery are not available to any other Publisher publications.

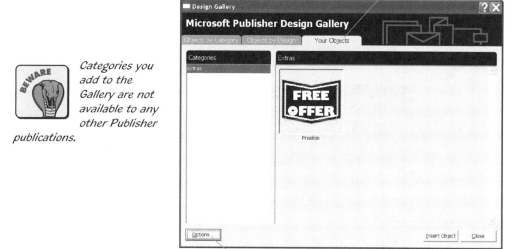

3 Click Options.

4 Click here.

To rename or delete a category, click it here:

Then select the Rename or Delete button and complete the dialog or message which launches.

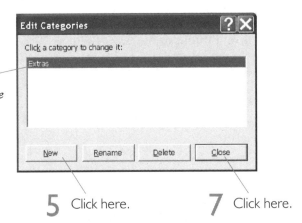

5 Click here.

7 Click here.

6 Name the category and click OK.

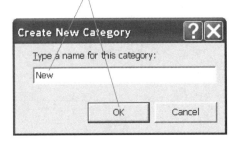

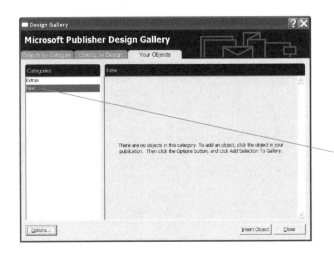

8 The new category has been added.

Creating a logo

Logos are everywhere! We see symbols of all kinds all the time. But to create the right look and put over the desired impression, designing and creating a corporate logo needs careful consideration.

To include a logo on every page of your document, you can place it on the master page as described on page 28.

Creating a logo using a wizard

1 Click the Design Gallery Object button on the Objects toolbar:

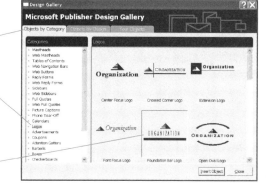

2 Click the Objects by Category tab.

3 In the Categories pane, click Logos.

You can make the presence of a logo more subtle by converting it into a watermark and placing it on the master page. Watermarks are described in the HOT TIP on page 121.

4 Double-click the logo you want.

5 Click this button: next to the inserted logo.

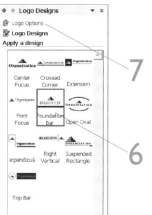

Logos you create here can't be incorporated into Personal Information Sets.

7 Click here to set other options (e.g. the number of lines of text).

6 Optional – click a new design to apply it.

Creating a headline

Headlines get noticed! Just make sure that the style you choose creates the right kind of tone and level of attention.

Creating a headline

1 Draw a text frame where you want the headline to appear.

2 Type the text for your headline.

If a main heading is followed by further subordinate headings, create a logical structure by using a hierarchy.

Format the main heading at the top of the hierarchy in larger, more bold type with a proportional space below. Then, for the remaining headings, progressively reduce the font size and proportional space as you move further down the hierarchy.

3 (Optional) Make any desired formatting changes to the font, font size and style, alignment, and so on.

4 (Optional) Include any desired text shading.

5 (Optional) Add a text frame border if desired. You can include a plain or decorative (BorderArt) border.

6 If you include a picture or other graphic objects with your headline, group the headline text and graphic objects together.

7 (Optional) Rotate the headline if desired. We rotated each chapter marker in this book 90 degrees to add contrast and to provide an easily recognizable start-of-chapter indicator.

Using a Design Gallery headline

Publisher includes several predesigned newsletter headings (mastheads) and title formats. To view these:

1 Click the Design Gallery Object button on the Objects toolbar:

2 Select the Objects by Category tab.

3 Under Categories, click Mastheads. You can then view and choose an option.

Using the BorderArt Gallery

Some shapes can't have BorderArt applied to them, like shapes drawn with the Oval tool or Custom Shapes tool. If the selected shape is not compatible with BorderArt, Publisher doesn't provide access to the BorderArt tab.

The BorderArt Gallery includes scores of plain and fancy borders, which you can use to transform an otherwise dull object into something more memorable. You can add BorderArt to any rectangular shapes you create in Publisher, including picture, text, table and WordArt frames.

Applying BorderArt

Double-click the relevant object. In the Format... dialog, click the BorderArt button.

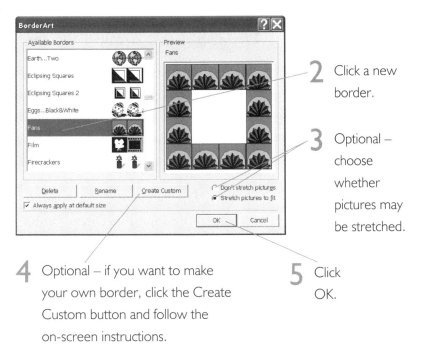

2 Click a new border.

3 Optional – choose whether pictures may be stretched.

4 Optional – if you want to make your own border, click the Create Custom button and follow the on-screen instructions.

5 Click OK.

Deleting a border

If you want to remove a border entirely, click None in step 2 above.

Wrapping text around a frame

Sometimes, you may want to flow ('wrap') text around a picture or other graphic object. Publisher provides several options to allow you to control how and when text wraps around an object. You can:

- Wrap text around a frame.

- Wrap text around the outline of a graphic object itself inside a frame.

- Customize text wrap precisely (around an object).

- Prevent text from wrapping.

Wrapping text around the frame of an object

1 Click the object around which you want to wrap text. To wrap text around several objects, select all the objects first.

2 If the object is layered – that is, if it is part of a stack of objects – press Alt+F6 to bring it to the front.

If you've chosen text wrap, but Publisher refuses to wrap text around a graphic object, the selected graphic may be set up as transparent. Try pressing Ctrl+T to make the graphic opaque.

3 Now, drag the object to the desired location over the text. When you release the mouse button, Publisher reflows the text around the object's rectangular frame.

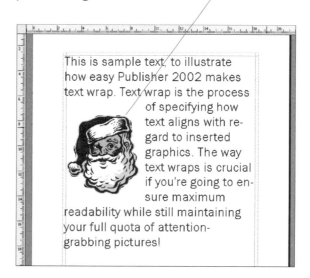

This is sample text, to illustrate how easy Publisher 2002 makes text wrap. Text wrap is the process of specifying how text aligns with regard to inserted graphics. The way text wraps is crucial if you're going to ensure maximum readability while still maintaining your full quota of attention-grabbing pictures!

Wrapping text around a picture

By wrapping text around the outline of a picture or WordArt object rather than its frame, you can create some stunning design results. This approach tends to work well when the graphic object contains some element of action, tension or emotion.

Customising text wrap

1 Click the picture or WordArt object to select it.

2 Click here in the Picture toolbar.

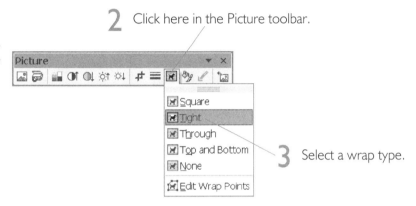

3 Select a wrap type.

'Tight' text wrap in action

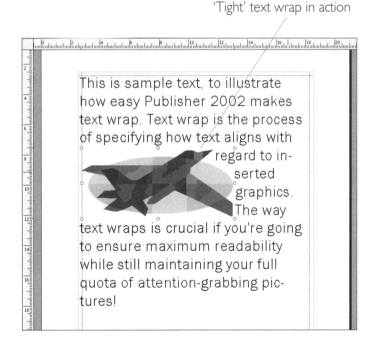

Changing the text wrap shape

Notice on the previous page that although we wrapped text around the image's outline, Publisher did not wrap text entirely around it. On this occasion, this was simply because the original image was determined by the shape you saw. However, Publisher provides the means to customize the text wrap and trace the perceived outline of the image more closely.

To turn off text wrap, right-click the object around which text is currently wrapping. Select Format Picture. In the Format Picture dialog, select the Layout tab. Under Wrapping style, click None. Click OK.

Editing text wrap

Click the picture or WordArt object to select it.

2 Click here in the Picture toolbar.

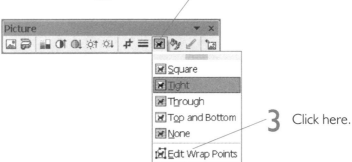

3 Click here.

To add a wrap point, hold down the Ctrl key while you click the boundary.

When reshaping the text wrap around a picture or WordArt object, if you want to delete a wrap point, hold down the Ctrl+Shift keys while you click it.

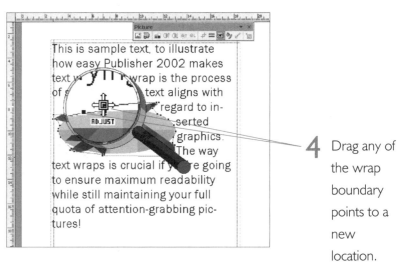

This is sample text, to illustrate how easy Publisher 2002 makes text wrap is the process of text aligns with regard to inserted graphics. The way text wraps is crucial if you're going to ensure maximum readability while still maintaining your full quota of attention-grabbing pictures!

4 Drag any of the wrap boundary points to a new location.

5 The text wrap is redefined.

Working with pages

This chapter examines the rich variety of options open to you when working with pages in Publisher. We explore the sometimes tricky business of matching colours; how to align objects using guides; how to change page size and margins; and go on to examine what implications this has for a publication. Headers and footers and their uses are also covered.

Finally, we show how to add, copy, change and delete entire pages.

Covers

Chapter Eleven

Using colour schemes

Colour schemes

A colour scheme is a special group of colours that are associated with a publication. Every Publisher document has a colour scheme, although you can define your own set if you wish. When you start a new publication, Publisher automatically applies a default colour scheme to it.

If you've already filled an object with a colour from the publication colour scheme, and decide to change the original colour in the colour scheme, Publisher changes the fill colours of any objects filled with the original colour to that of the new colour.

Standard colour schemes that Publisher applies to new publications are carefully chosen so that the relative colours match together. You can design your own custom colour scheme if you feel the standard colour scheme is not right for your purposes.

Applying a new colour scheme

Perform the steps below:

Not all Publisher colours belong to colour schemes – see page 52.

1 Click the Color Schemes command in the Format menu.

If no colour schemes are available, choose Tools, Commercial Printing Tools, Color Printing. In the dialog, select Composite RGB. Click OK.

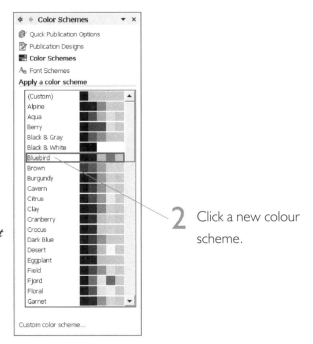

2 Click a new colour scheme.

3 Each colour from the old colour scheme is replaced with the corresponding new colour.

Creating a custom colour scheme

You can create an entirely new colour scheme or replace perhaps only one or two colours from an existing scheme by carrying out the steps below:

1 Click the Color Schemes command in the Format menu.

 To fill an object with a colour from the scheme colour set, first click the object to select it. Next, on the Formatting toolbar click the Fill Color button. Then under the Scheme Colors category, click the new colour you want.

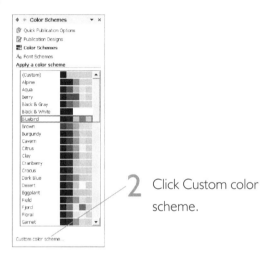

2 Click Custom color scheme.

 To print a sample of all the colour schemes, select the Standard tab. Click the Print color sampler button – printing is immediate.

 To save your colour scheme, click here: and complete the Save Scheme dialog.

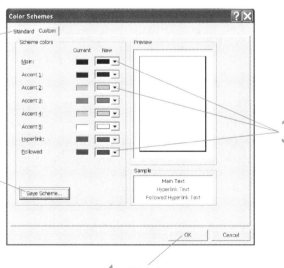

3 For each colour (or selectively) click its New arrow and select a new colour in the list.

4 Click here.

Viewing a two-page spread

Many multi-page publications, like the one shown below for instance, require printing on both sides of the paper. When you're viewing a publication on the screen with two pages side by side – just like this book – Publisher considers this form of layout as a two-page spread.

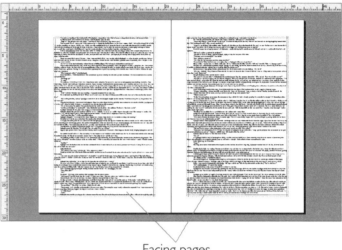

Facing pages

If a publication has three or more pages, you can opt to view facing pages side by side, as a two-page spread. To do this, open the View menu and click Two-Page Spread. To switch back to Single Page view, open the View menu and click the command again to clear the tick mark.

Two-page spread design considerations

When establishing the structure of a document containing facing pages, it's a good idea to apply some special consideration to the design. For example, consider the following:

- Documents with facing pages generally need wider inner margins to allow for the folding or binding after the document is printed.

- Decide whether you want the left and right pages to look the same in terms of layout, or whether you want each to mirror the other (as shown above).

Changing page size

Your publication page size can be different to the paper page size. The paper page size is the size of paper you choose to print on, for example A4. The publication page size is the size you specify for your publication. For example, you might create a size A3 publication; but this could be made up from printed A4 sheets (called tiles), which you could then photocopy or take to a printer to create the final product.

Changing the printer paper size

1 Choose the Page Setup command in the File menu.

Remember, if you design a publication for one printer, but later decide to set the document up for another printer, you may have to carry out a considerable amount of work correcting the page layout for the new target printer.

2 Click the Printer & Paper tab.

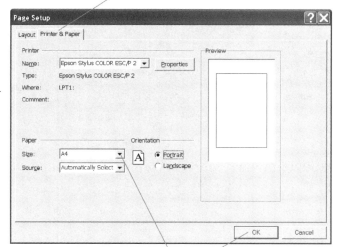

Select a page orientation, too, by clicking Portrait (vertical) or Landscape (sideways on).

3 Click the arrow, select a new paper size in the list then click OK.

Changing the publication page size

Re step 3 on the right – alternatively, select Custom and type in your own measurements in the Width and Height fields.

1 Perform step 1 above.

2 In step 2, select the Layout tab.

3 In step 3, select a page size in the Publication type field.

Changing page margins

Page margins are the spaces at the top, bottom, left and right edges of your pages, which are outside of the area where you place text or graphics. Publisher identifies the inner edge of page margins with non-printing dotted lines.

When you start a new document, Publisher applies a single column with 2.5cm margins around the page. However, you can change top, bottom, left and right margins. Carry out the steps below to change the size of margins:

If you change page margins after laying out a publication, you may have to realign text and graphic objects. Therefore, set margin sizes at the start of your new publication.

| Open the Arrange menu and click the Layout Guides command.

When setting margins, you need to ensure you don't go into your printer's non-printing region (see also page 157).

To determine this, launch WordPad. Choose File, Page Setup. Delete the existing margin settings. New settings appear; these are your printer's minimums. Make a note of these settings and use them as limits in Publisher.

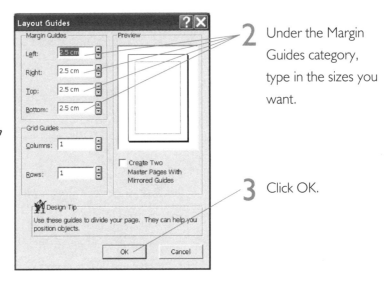

2 Under the Margin Guides category, type in the sizes you want.

3 Click OK.

Displaying and hiding margin guides

If you can't see a margin guide that you know should be there, it may be hidden behind opaque objects.

Alternatively, if you can't see any guides at all, the Boundaries and Guides command in the View menu may be switched on. To re-display page margins and other guides and boundaries, untick Boundaries and Guides in the View menu.

Using layout and ruler guides

Layout guides form a useful grid structure.

Publisher provides layout and ruler guides to help you align objects accurately on the page. Each layout guide you insert is repeated on every page in a publication and appears as a blue or pink dotted line, whereas you add ruler guides to individual pages only when you need them. Publisher displays ruler guides as green dotted lines.

Setting layout guides

Use layout guides when you want to create a framework of rows and columns on which to plan your publication.

1 Open the Arrange menu and click the Layout Guides command.

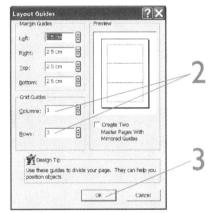

2 Enter the number of rows and columns you want here.

3 Click OK to apply your chosen layout guides.

To align a ruler guide exactly with a ruler mark, choose Arrange, Snap. Make sure Snap to Ruler Marks is ticked (if it isn't, click it). Then, drag a ruler guide to the ruler mark you want.

Applying ruler guides

1 Hold down the Shift key, then place the mouse pointer on the horizontal or vertical ruler.

To move or delete a ruler guide, hold down Shift and place the mouse pointer over the ruler guide you want to move or delete until you see the Adjust pointer. Then drag the guide where you want it or off the page if you want to delete it.

2 When the mouse pointer changes to the Adjust symbol, drag the ruler guide onto the page where you want it.

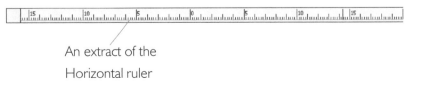

An extract of the Horizontal ruler

Snapping to guides and rulers

Earlier, we looked at how guides help you line up objects. To align them accurately, though, Publisher provides the Snap To commands. If these are switched on, when you move an object near a layout or ruler guide (or another object), Publisher applies a kind of magnetic pull to the object, 'snapping' it into position.

If the Snap to Guides command is switched on, Publisher will still snap objects to guides even if guides are hidden.

Switching the Snap To commands on and off

You can turn the Snap To commands on or off simply by clicking the desired command. When a Snap To command is switched on, Publisher places a tick next to it. To turn a Snap To command off, simply untick the desired command.

To snap several objects at the same time, select all the objects you want to snap, by holding down Shift while you click each object you want. Next, place the mouse pointer over one of the selected objects until you see the Move symbol. Then drag the objects to the desired location and snap into position.

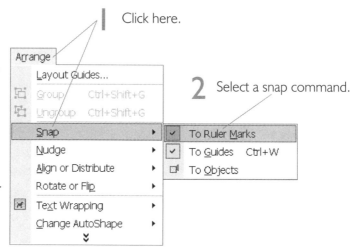

Click here.

2 Select a snap command.

How Snap To affects objects already in position

Changing the status of a Snap To command does not affect objects already positioned before you chose the command. If you want those objects to snap also, simply drag them into position.

The precedence rule

If all three Snap To commands are switched on when you're aligning objects, Publisher applies the precedence rule:

*   First, Publisher tries to snap to the nearest guide.

*   If no guide is near, Publisher tries to snap to an object.

*   If no object exists, Publisher snaps to the nearest ruler mark.

Using headers and footers

You can arrange for Publisher to ignore headers, footers and other items on specific pages. This feature is particularly useful if you don't want headers and footers to appear on the first page of your publication. In normal (non-Master) view, simply move to the page you want, then click Ignore Master Page in the View menu.

Headers and footers contain text and graphic information about your publication, like page numbers, publication or section titles, horizontal lines and so on. Headers are placed at the top of a page and footers at the bottom. Remember, you place the objects you want to repeat on every page on the Master page – Publisher automatically does this with headers/footers.

Adding headers and footers

1 Choose the Header and Footer command in the View menu.

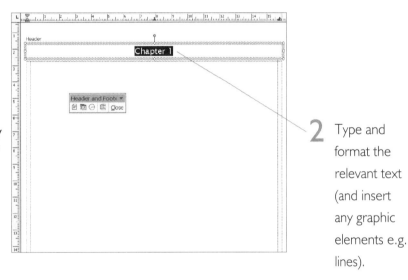

When adding page numbers, if you type a number instead of inserting the page number marker while in the Master page, Publisher places that same number on every page when you return to normal view.

2 Type and format the relevant text (and insert any graphic elements e.g. lines).

Inserting page numbers

To quickly delete a header, footer, or page number marker, first move to the Master page. Then right-click the header, footer, or page number text frame to select it. In the floating menu, click Delete Object. Finally, press Ctrl+M.

1 Click in the header/footer where you want the page number to go.

2 Click this button: [#] in the Header and Footer toolbar.

3 Publisher inserts a hash symbol (#) as the page number marker.

4 Press Ctrl+M – page number markers appear as page numbers in normal view.

Adding headers and footers to facing pages

To include headers and footers in publications containing facing pages, like this book, first make sure you're viewing both pages side by side. If not, click the Two-Page Spread command in the View menu. Then do the following:

1 Choose the Header and Footer command in the View menu.

2 Type and format the relevant header/footer text (and insert any graphic elements e.g. lines).

3 On the Arrange menu, click the Layout Guides command.

4 In the Layout Guides dialog box, select Create Two Master Pages With Mirrored Guides.

5 Click the OK button to place the mirrored headers or footers on the pages. If you want to change either the left or right header or footer, you can edit the desired header or footer now:

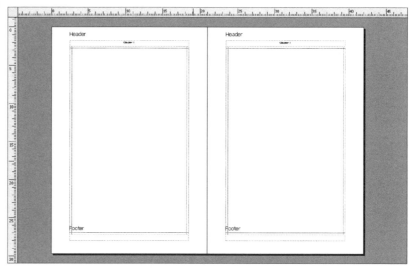

6 Press Ctrl+M to return to normal view.

Adding a page

If you're working on a two-page spread publication, it's easier to maintain the publication page pattern by adding/deleting pages in even numbers.

You can easily add pages anywhere in your document. To add pages, first use the Page Navigation/control buttons at the lower left of the Publisher window to move to the page where you want to add extra pages. Next, open the Insert menu and click the Page command. Then carry out the steps below:

To delete a page, move to it. In the Edit menu, click Delete Page. (You can't add or delete pages while you're viewing the Master page.)

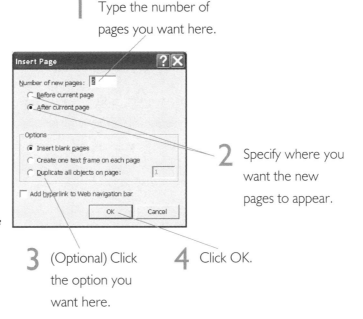

1 Type the number of pages you want here.

2 Specify where you want the new pages to appear.

Re step 3 – select Duplicate all objects on page (and then enter the relevant page number) to insert all objects on the specified page into the new pages you create.

3 (Optional) Click the option you want here.

4 Click OK.

When you insert pages, Publisher copies any text, graphics or guides placed on the Master page to your new pages.

If you can't see the Master page layout guides

If you've inserted your new pages but can't see the layout guides you placed on the Master page, you may have clicked the Create one text frame on each page option under the Options category in the Insert Page dialog box. This causes Publisher to place a new text frame on top of any guides.

If there are text or graphic objects on the page(s) you are deleting which you want to keep, drag the items you want onto the non-printing workspace area before you delete the page(s).

The new text frame should be transparent, but as it isn't select it and press Ctrl+T to remedy this. (Or simply delete the frame if you don't want it.)

Changing the look of a page

If you want a border to appear on every page in your publication, create it on the Master page (see page 28 for more information about the Master page).

Placing a border around a page

Placing a border around a page is similar to simply drawing a box. However, while deciding the size of your border box, make sure you don't draw in your printer's unprintable region (see chapter 12). Perform the following steps:

1 Click the Rectangle tool on the Objects toolbar:

2 Move the mouse pointer to where you want the uppermost left corner of your border to appear.

3 Hold down the left mouse button while you drag the mouse diagonally towards the lower-most right corner of the page. Release the button when you see the desired size.

4 Click the Formatting toolbar Line/Border Style button:

5 On the floating menu that appears, click the More Lines command.

6 In the Line section of the Format... dialog, choose the options you want then click the OK button.

Filling a page with a colour or pattern

When filling a page with a pattern, it's usually best to stick with larger text sizes and clear, bold fonts like Arial: this aids clarity.

See pages 52–53 for help with applying colours and patterns.

1 Perform the steps above to draw a rectangular border around the page (or the area you want to fill).

2 On the Formatting toolbar, click the Fill Color button arrow:

3 From the floating menu that appears, select a colour. Or choose Fill Effects to apply a pattern, then complete the Fill Effects dialog and click OK.

4 On the menu bar, click Arrange to open the Arrange menu, then click the Send to Back command.

Checking/previewing your work

You're almost ready to print or publish, but before you do we examine how to use Publisher's powerful document-checking tools (and Print Preview) to help ensure the text and layout of your publication are perfect.

Covers

Chapter Twelve

Checking text spacing

After you've entered text into a publication, Publisher can check your text for any extra spaces between words. As you type, it's easy to insert two or more spaces between words without realising. This can make text look unsightly, especially if it's justified.

To search your text for double (or more) spaces after words, first click to the left of the first character in the text frame you want to check. Next, open the Edit menu and click the Replace command. Then carry out the steps below:

1 Click in the Find what field and press the Spacebar twice to enter two spaces.

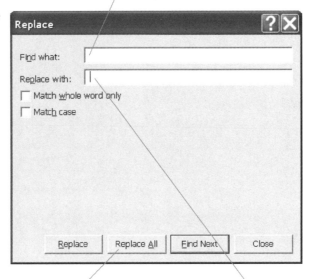

3 Click the Replace All button.

2 In the Replace with box, press the Spacebar once.

4 Repeat step 3 as often as necessary, until all superfluous double spaces have been removed.

5 Repeat the procedure for all the text frames you want to check.

Correcting errors while you type

Using AutoCorrect

While entering text, it's easy to make common errors. For example, we may develop a habit of typing 'nad' when we really meant to type the word 'and'. Publisher, however, includes AutoCorrect – a clever facility to help automatically correct these sorts of errors.

To gain a better understanding of how AutoCorrect works, make a list of words or phrases that you often misspell, making sure that you write each word or phrase exactly as you often misspell it. Using the example above you would write 'nad' for 'and.' Then:

Whenever you're typing text in Publisher, try to get into the habit of being aware when you enter text incorrectly. Once a pattern is identified, that's the ideal time to enter it into Publisher's AutoCorrect feature while the event is fresh in your mind. Then you can forget about it knowing that AutoCorrect will identify and correct any future errors of this type.

1 Open the Tools menu and click AutoCorrect Options.

2 Make sure Replace text as you type is ticked.

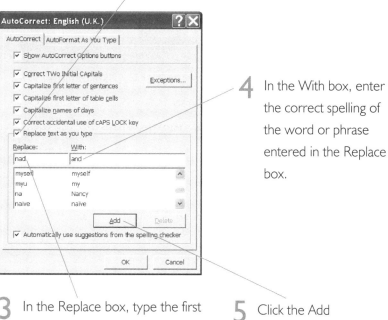

4 In the With box, enter the correct spelling of the word or phrase entered in the Replace box.

3 In the Replace box, type the first word or phrase on your list that you often misspell.

5 Click the Add button.

6 Repeat steps 3–5 for all the other words on your list, then click OK.

Preventing AutoCorrect misspelling special words or acronyms

Some words can be spelt in several ways. The word 'reference' for example is often abbreviated to 'ref.' – normally, AutoCorrect would ensure a capital letter occurs after a full stop is entered, but you wouldn't want this here. If you want to use a particular spelling, you can ensure AutoCorrect does what you want in these special circumstances.

Perform the steps below:

To replace computer-standard quotes or hyphens with the more professional typesetter's equivalents, do the following. First, click AutoCorrect in the Tools menu. Then in the AutoCorrect dialog box, click the AutoFormat As You Type tab. Make sure "Straight quotes" with "smart quotes" is ticked. Click OK.

To enter other exceptions, click the Other Corrections tab. In the Don't correct box, enter a word whose spelling you don't want Publisher to correct. Click Add then OK.

1 Open the Tools menu and click AutoCorrect Options.

2 Click the Exceptions button.

3 Select the First Letter tab.

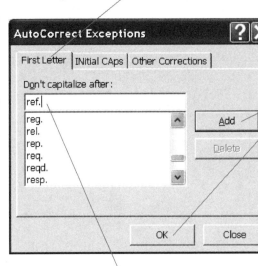

5 Click Add then OK.

4 Type the word (inc. the full stop) after which you don't want Publisher to capitalise.

Spell-checking

Publisher 2002 lets you check text in two ways:

- on-the-fly, as you type in text

- separately, after the text has been entered into frames

Checking text on-the-fly

This is the default. When automatic checking is in force, Publisher 2002 flags words it doesn't agree with, using a wavy red underline. If the word or phrase is wrong, right-click in it. Then carry out steps 1, 2 or 3:

To disable on-the-fly checking, pull down the Tools menu and click Spelling, Spelling Options. Untick Check spelling as you type and click OK.

To set the language of the text you check (this determines the dictionaries Publisher uses), select the relevant text. Choose Tools, Language, Set Language. Select the language you want – e.g. English (UK) – and click OK.

Re step 2 – you have an extra option. Click Add to Dictionary if:

1. the flagged word is correct, and;

2. you want Publisher to remember it in future spell-checks.

1 Publisher often provides a list of alternatives. If one is correct, click it; the flagged word is replaced with the correct version.

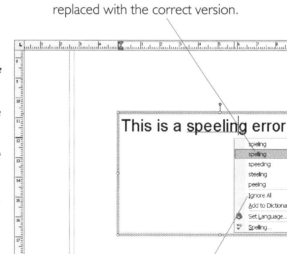

2 To have the flagged word stand, click Ignore All.

3 If the flagged word is wrong but can't be corrected now, click Spelling and complete the resulting dialog (see overleaf).

You can use a keyboard shortcut to run a spell-check: press F7.

To spell-check all text frames in the publication, tick Check all stories.

If you're correcting a spelling error, you have two further options:

- *Click Add to have the flagged word stored in CUSTOM.DIC (see above), or;*

- *Click Change All to have Publisher substitute its suggestion for all future instances of the flagged word*

Checking text separately

To check all the text within the active text or table frame in one go, click in the frame. Pull down the Tools menu and click Spelling, Spelling. Publisher 2002 starts spell-checking the frame from the beginning. When it encounters a word or phrase it doesn't recognise, Publisher flags it and produces a special dialog (see below). Usually, it provides alternative suggestions; if one of these is correct, you can opt to have it replace the flagged word. You can do this singly (i.e. just this instance is replaced) or globally (where all future instances – within the current checking session – are replaced).

Alternatively, you can have Publisher ignore *this* instance of the flagged word, ignore *all* future instances of the word or add the word to CUSTOM.DIC (see the tips). After this, Publisher resumes checking.

Carry out step 1 below, then follow step 2. Alternatively, carry out step 3 or 4.

1 If one of the suggestions here is correct, click it, then follow step 2.

3 Click Ignore to ignore just this instance.

4 Click Ignore All to ignore all future instances.

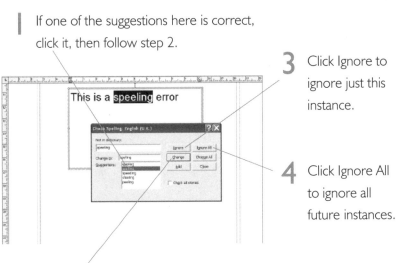

2 Click Change to replace this instance.

Searching for synonyms

Publisher 2002 lets you search for synonyms while you're editing the active text frame. You do this by calling up Publisher's resident Thesaurus. The Thesaurus categorises words into meanings; each meaning is allocated various synonyms from which you can choose.

As a bonus, the Thesaurus also supplies antonyms. For example, if you look up 'good' in the Thesaurus (as below), Publisher lists 'poor' as an antonym.

You can use a keyboard shortcut to run the Thesaurus: press Shift+F7.

Using the Thesaurus

First, select the word for which you require a synonym or antonym (or simply position the insertion point within it). Pull down the Tools menu and click Language, Thesaurus. Now do the following:

The selected word appears here

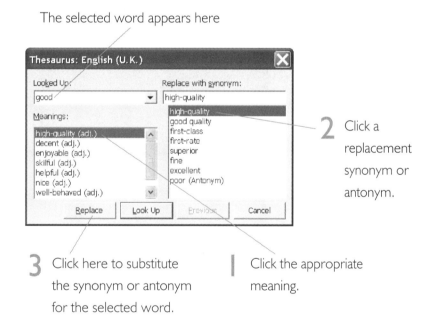

2 Click a replacement synonym or antonym.

3 Click here to substitute the synonym or antonym for the selected word.

1 Click the appropriate meaning.

Using the Design Checker

Publisher provides the Design Checker for checking the layout of a publication, and tries to identify problems that may prevent the publication from printing normally.

For example, in the dialog box on the facing page, Publisher has identified an object placed on the non-printing area of the page.

You can check specific pages or an entire publication.

Running the Design Checker

1 In the Tools menu, choose Design Checker.

2 By default, Publisher checks the entire publication. If you don't want this, select Pages and enter a page range.

Leave Check master pages ticked if you want Design Checker to include the master page.

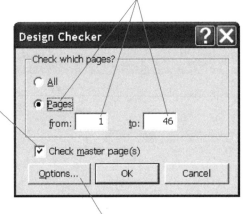

3 Or you can tell Publisher to check only for specific problems. Click the Options button then tick the features you want, followed by OK.

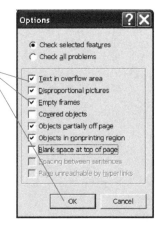

4 If Publisher detects a layout problem, it displays an appropriate dialog box.

7 Click Ignore (singly) or Ignore All (globally) to move on to the next problem

The Design Checker dialog box stays on the screen until you click Close or the check is finished. If this, or any other dialog box, is blocking a clear view of your publication, drag the dialog box Title bar away.

Design Checker

Problem:
This object is in the printer's nonprinting region.

Suggestions:
If this object is not part of your design, move, delete, or resize the object so that it fits on the page. For more information, click Explain.

Ignore   Ignore All

Continue   Close

Explain...

6 Go back to your publication and fix the problem, then click Continue.

5 (Optional) Click the Explain button to see more details about the current problem.

After a document has been checked, Publisher displays a message. Click OK to close down Design Checker.

A word about your printer's nonprinting region

Most printers aren't able to print exactly to the edge of the paper. This unprintable area varies from printer to printer. For how to determine what your printer's nonprinting area is, see the DON'T FORGET tip on page 142.

Using Print Preview

Publisher 2002 provides a special view mode called Print Preview. This displays the active publication exactly as it will look when printed. Use Print Preview as a final check just before you print your publication.

You can customise the way Print Preview displays your document. For example, you can:

To specify the number of pages displayed, click this button in the toolbar:

* zoom in or out on the active page

* specify how many pages display

Launching Print Preview

Pull down the File menu and click Print Preview. This is the result:

In the drop-down list, select a view option – e.g. 1x3 sheets:

Print Preview toolbar

To zoom in or out (as appropriate) left-click once.

Magnifying cursor

Press Esc to leave Print Preview.

Printing and emailing a publication

If you're not interested in publishing to the web, printing a paper-based publication is the crowning glory of all your efforts. In this chapter, we explain how to print a publication and examine the main options open to you when you print. We also take a closer look at the implications of using an outside printing organisation, including special precautions you can take to help ensure your publication is output exactly as you intended.

Finally, we explain how to send a publication by email.

Covers

Chapter Thirteen

Printing the date and time

If you're intending to print several drafts of a publication, it's useful to know when you printed each draft. Publisher provides a command which inserts the date and/or time in the publication.

To insert the date or time, click in the text frame where you want it to appear or draw a new text frame. Next, open the Insert menu and click Date and Time. Then carry out the steps below:

1 Under the Available formats category, click the date or time format you want.

By inserting the date and/or time, you can keep a permanent log of all your printouts. This can be useful when verifying dates and times with printers and work colleagues.

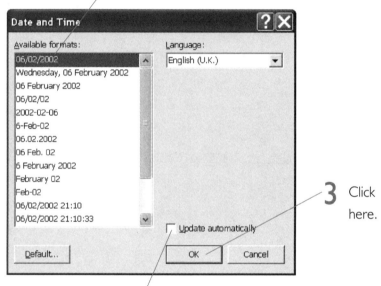

3 Click here.

You can also include times/ dates in a table frame. In this context, Publisher considers a table to simply be a more formalised text frame.

2 To have the time/date automatically updated each time you open or print the publication, tick this.

Printing on special paper

Providing you've not chosen to use an outside printer (see the DON'T FORGET tip) you can still create an attractive, professional, coloured finish to your publications, without incurring the higher costs often associated with using several colours. You could try using pre-printed coloured paper stock.

If you've chosen to print to an 'outside' commercial printer, the Special Paper command in the View menu may not be available.

PaperDirect (www.paperdirect.com) is a company that produces a range of coloured papers and patterns. Publisher includes 42 coloured styles which you can use. You choose a style, add the text and graphics you want, then simply print.

Using special paper

Open the View menu and click Special Paper. Then perform the steps below:

Printing using the special paper option is an excellent way to create a consistent and stylish corporate identity including business cards, compliment slips, letterheads, and so on, at a modest price.

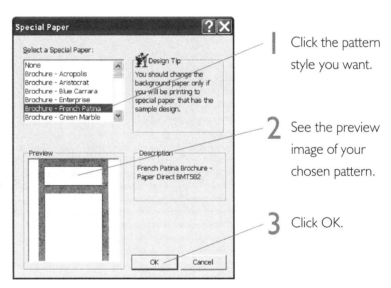

1 Click the pattern style you want.

2 See the preview image of your chosen pattern.

3 Click OK.

4 Add text/graphics then print as explained overleaf when ready.

Disabling special paper use

1 Open the View menu and click Special Paper.

2 Under the Select a Special Paper category, click None followed by OK.

Printing to a desktop printer

When you started your publication, you established which printer you want to use to print your publication.

Printing a publication whose size is smaller than the paper you're printing to

You can change or specify further choices for your printer, including paper size, graphics and colour options (if applicable) by clicking the Properties button and making your choices in the dialog boxes.

1 Make sure your printer is online and ready to print.

2 Open the File menu and click Print.

3 Carry out any of steps 2–7 on page 164.

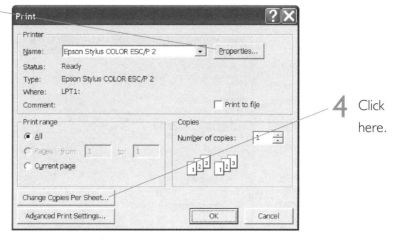

To print on non-standard-sized paper, first open the File menu and click Page Setup. Select the Printer & Paper tab. Under the Paper category, click the paper size you want. Click OK.

4 Click here.

5 In the Small Publication Print Options dialog, select Print one copy per sheet.

6 Alternatively, select Print multiple copies per sheet and enter Side Margin, Top Margin, Horizontal Gap and/or Vertical Gap values:

After step 6, click OK twice.

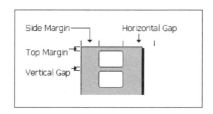

Printing a publication whose size is larger than the paper you're printing to

When a publication is larger than the paper it prints on, Publisher 'tiles' it (i.e. prints it in overlapping segments).

1 Follow steps 1–3 on the facing page.

2 In the Print dialog, click the Change Overlap button.

4 To print all the tiles, select Print Entire Page. Then (optionally) redefine the amount by which tiles overlap each other.

Re step 3 – this prints the tile which is nearest to the ruler origin (the blank square where the vertical and horizontal rulers intersect). If this isn't what you want, carry out the following procedure before you launch the Print dialog. Hold down Ctrl then:

Drag the blank square to the location from which you want to print the tile.

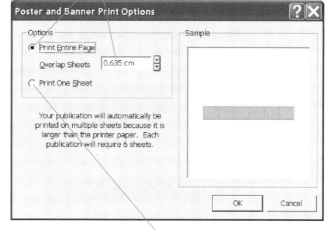

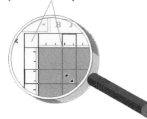

3 To print one tile, click here (but see the HOT TIP).

Using the Print Troubleshooter

If your publication doesn't print the way you expect it to, or won't print, you can use Publisher's Print Troubleshooter. To have this launch each time you print, pull down the Tools menu and select Options. In the Options dialog, select the Print tab. Tick Automatically display print troubleshooter.

...cont'd

To quickly print an entire publication without displaying the
Print dialog box and without changing any default print options, click the Print button on the Standard toolbar:

Advanced print options

1 Follow steps 1–2 on page 162.

3 In a multipage publication, click here to choose which
pages you want to print, then enter a range.

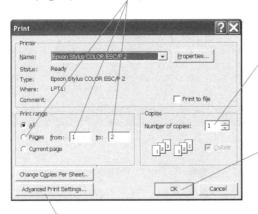

2 Optional – enter the number of copies you want printed.

8 Click here.

4 Optional – click here.

5 (Optional) Choose the options you want here.

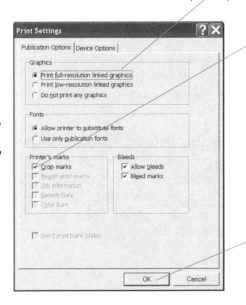

If you decide to print your publication to a file for the use of a
commercial printer, discuss this option in detail with your printing service first.

6 Optional – crop marks help you trim a publication when it's smaller or larger than the paper size to which you're printing. Tick this to include crop marks on your printouts.

7 Click here.

Using a commercial printing service

If you intend to deliver your publication to your print shop in Publisher's own format (assuming they support this), you can copy the files using the Pack and Go Wizard. Choose File, Pack and Go, Take to a Commercial Printing Service.

(This is in many ways a better option than saving to PostScript format.)

Before you submit your publication to a print shop, establish with them which type of printing to use. Then choose Tools, Commercial Printing Tools, Color Printing and do the following, as appropriate:

* *For Black and white – select Single color publication*

* *For Process colour – select Process colors (CMYK) then evaluate any colour changes in your publication*

* *For spot colour – select Spot color(s) then add/ modify/delete the relevant colours*

* *Mix and match spot/ process colour. Choose spot colour (above) then select a colour. Click Modify. In the Colors dialog, select the Custom tab. In the Color model field, select PANTONE. Select a PANTONE swatch and confirm your actions*

To produce many copies of your publication, or to produce a better quality finish than you can achieve from your desktop printer, consider using a commercial printing service. You can hand a printed master copy to your printer; deliver your publication on disk in Publisher format; print to a PostScript file; or email your publication to a print shop. However, speak to your print shop first to find out exactly what they require.

Printing quality and resolution issues

If you're using a commercial printer, you can use:

* Spot colour: suitable when all colours and shades in a publication are made up from one or two 'real' colours. This option provides high-quality output which can be relatively inexpensive. Use spot colours particularly for headings, borders and logos, or for special ink finishes.

* Process colours: ideal if your publication contains colour photographs or more than two shades of colour other than black and white, or if it requires very high resolution. But remember, this option can be particularly expensive.

* Black and white with shades of grey: here printing quality can be excellent and cost can be quite reasonable. But it may be worthwhile shopping around.

* A combination of spot and process colours.

Printing to a file

If your print shop wants your publication as a PostScript file (for example, if it only uses Macintosh computers), do the following:

1. After saving your file in Publisher, choose File, Save As.

2. In the Save as type field, select PostScript (*.ps). Then name the file, select a destination drive/folder and click Save.

3. Complete the Save as PostScript File dialog (e.g. select a PostScript output device) then click Save.

4. Send the file to your chosen printer (on disk or via email).

Establishing trapping values

Overprinting prints black or dark coloured text and objects on top of any lighter coloured background colour. By default, Publisher overprints imported pictures, lines, fills and dark coloured text.

In commercial colour printing, while a publication is being printed, the paper or printing plates can shift or stretch slightly and misregistration of the inks can occur. However, Publisher allows you to compensate for these effects by using two key techniques: trapping and overprinting (see the tips for more information).

Publisher can apply trapping only when you print colour separations; separations are used only when you choose process- or spot-colour printing (see page 165 for more information). When you start a new publication, Publisher does not apply any trapping. If you decide to use trapping, you can use the default setting suggested by Publisher or you can apply your own (but see the HOT TIP). Publisher follows its own set of sophisticated rules to determine trapping values.

Re step 2 – only use trapping if your print shop asks for it (if so, it may well be preferable to get them to supply the relevant settings rather than use Publisher's defaults).

Applying automatic trapping

Open the Tools menu and choose Commercial Printing Tools, Trapping, Preferences.

Where two different coloured objects meet, trapping works by extending the lighter colour so that it overlaps slightly into the darker coloured object. This ensures that no gaps appear where there should be none and so avoids any misregistration.

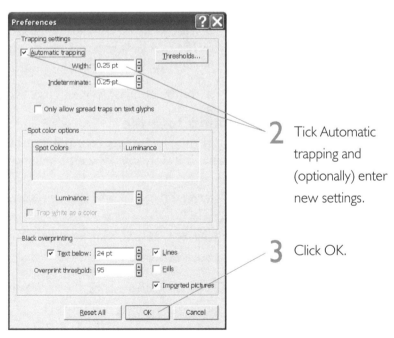

2 Tick Automatic trapping and (optionally) enter new settings.

3 Click OK.

Embedding fonts in a publication

If you're planning to print your publication via a print shop or on another computer, the fonts you've used may not be installed. However, by embedding the fonts you use you can ensure that they're available to any commercial printing service or on any other PC.

Publisher can embed TrueType fonts in the current publication when the fonts are already installed in Windows and providing the fonts you use allow embedding. However, Publisher embeds *only* TrueType fonts although all the fonts included with Publisher automatically have full embedding rights.

Not all fonts are licensed to support embedding.

Embedding fonts in a publication

When you use the Pack and Go Wizard, by default, Publisher turns on embedding. However, you can choose not to embed fonts (although it's safer to leave this option enabled): simply deselect Embed TrueType fonts.

Embedding fonts materially increases file size. As a result:

- *Don't use too many fonts*
- *Check with your print shop: if they have any of the fonts you've used, don't embed them (see step 3)*

1 Open the Tools menu and choose Commercial Printing Tools, Fonts.

2 To embed TrueType fonts when you save a publication, tick this.

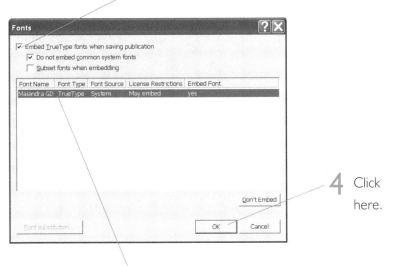

4 Click here.

3 To change the embed status of a specific font, click it then select Don't Embed.

Sending your publication by email

You can also send a publication within the body of an email itself. In step 2, select Mail Recipient in the submenu. Address the email and click Send This Page.

Email is an ideal medium to use if you want to pass on or obtain important information relatively quickly.

Sending publications as email attachments

1 Make sure that you've saved your publication.

2 Pull down the File menu and click Send To, Mail Recipient (as Attachment).

It's advisable to print separations or a composite of your publication and give this to your print shop for verification. This ensures that colours are printing correctly.

Ensure you've selected spot or process colours (page 165). Press Ctrl+P. Select a Separations option (Print composite prints on 1 page, Print separations prints one page in black and white for each colour used). Click OK.

3 Address and complete the email, as usual, then click Send.

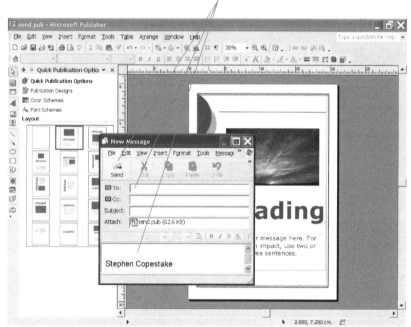

You can reduce the amount of time needed to email a publication by using a program like WinZip to compress your publication before sending it. WinZip is shareware and available from most shareware vending websites. (Alternatively, use Windows XP's inbuilt compression – see your XP documentation).

Now zip your file and attach it to an email in your email program, in the usual way.

4 Your publication is sent as an attachment to your email message.

Creating a compelling website

In this final chapter we introduce and define the Internet and World Wide Web, and explain how you can create, modify, check and preview your website using Publisher's powerful yet easy-to-use website creation tools. We also describe how to insert and use forms. Then, when you're ready, we explain how to publish your website to the web and edit it in Internet Explorer.

Covers

Chapter Fourteen

Introducing the World Wide Web

You can send and receive information anywhere across the globe using one of the many free ISPs that are now available, for only the cost of local phone calls. Or you can use one of the several schemes where users pay a small additional monthly charge for unmetered access.

The Internet and the World Wide Web (WWW): words we often hear used interchangeably, but which in fact are not the same thing. While the Internet is a network that allows data to be carried between computers across the globe, the WWW simply provides an easy way of viewing and navigating the data that is stored on the tens of thousands of computers that make up the Internet.

Today, anyone – companies, organisations and individuals – with access to a PC, modem and hence to the Internet, can advertise or market themselves and their products on the web. Companies, small and large, can advertise to up to 55 million people worldwide – and this number is rising daily – for mere pence per day.

The web provides a new avenue to enable any organisation to attract customers worldwide, 24 hours a day, at low cost. Individuals can also set up their own 'Home Page', simply as a means to contact other individuals who share the same interests, or to advertise their skills, their wares, and to display their CVs to potential employers.

Compared to a paper-based advertising budget, your web budget can be small by comparison, yet may be just as effective – or even more so – while being less wasteful in resources.

The Internet and the web, even now are rich in new possibilities and nobody *really* knows where the web is going. But Microsoft have ensured, with Publisher 2002, that their publishing product will not be left behind. Publisher's web tools are refreshingly easy to use and simple to apply, yet are powerful and flexible. The remainder of this chapter explains how you can produce your own web pages in Publisher quickly and effectively.

The web is growing quickly. Globally, well over 200 million subscribers are now online – 1 billion are expected by 2005 (source: Motorola 1999 survey)!

The benefits of having a website

For businesses, organisations and clubs

A carefully designed, compelling website can provide a powerful way in which to keep in contact with a wide range of potential customers, existing customers or members. Once your clients have recorded or 'bookmarked' your website, you can easily keep in contact with them using web promotions, features, special offers and so on. Here are some of the more important benefits:

On your Home or Index page, tell your visitors to bookmark the page immediately, so they can always find your site again easily.

- Contact thousands of prospects cheaply using only your well designed website and the awesome power of email.

- Easy access to a vast and wide range of information: there's something for everyone on the Internet.

- An international, global audience: you're no longer constrained by national boundaries.

The Internet is a great leveller: both small and large firms can market themselves on a level playing field.

- The Internet is an ideal, low-cost way to test new products or ideas.

- Some products may only be profitable for the small business when sold on the Internet.

- Most Internet users have disposable income (computer, modem, software, credit card, etc.): this means you can have access to a defined affluent customer base who have the capacity to spend money – if won over.

For individuals

You can establish a web page simply because you want to prove you can do it and the fact that you have that option. This is as good a reason as any other. Some individuals, however, may want to enhance their careers, impress their boss or even provide an all-singing, all-dancing CV-oriented website, ready for those all-important job interviews...

For many businesses, information is the new currency, and the web is now one of the most powerful tools to gain access to the most up-to-date information quickly.

The main theme to remember, if you want to build up *and* maintain the number of visitors, is: provide something unique, valuable or attractive on your website.

Avoiding web page design pitfalls

Creating a website is no longer a difficult undertaking. A wide variety of software tools are available to help you, including:

If you publish material on the web that you don't own, ensure that you have copyright or permission to do so, to avoid possible costly litigation.

- *FrontPage* from Microsoft.

- Shareware offerings like Luckman's *WebEdit Pro.*

But it's easy to get carried away by adding components that may do little to add to the value and useability of a website.

Design for success

For businesses however, effective website design is crucial. The following is all-important:

Don't apply watermarks to web pages. Why? The watermarked graphic in the background will almost certainly slow down the download speed of your web page – many visitors won't wait too long.

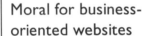

Moral for business-oriented websites	Every single component that goes to make up the site must contribute in some way to sales

This can scarcely be overstated: it's so important. Ruthlessly cut out every excess word, component or anything that does not really contribute to your website's theme. And particularly avoid using larger graphics that take a long time to download! Through applying a little thought and consideration, you can create an effective, compelling website that captures your prospects' attention and compels them to buy.

Aim to have your website listed in the top 20% of sites found by the major search engines – it can be done! Research on the web how others – often one-person organisations – are doing just that right now.

Learn about how to avoid web page design pitfalls in 'Web Page Design in easy steps' in this series.

The great thing about the Internet is how individuals and small organisations can project an image as good as – and sometimes better than – those of the larger organisations investing hundreds of thousands of pounds a year into their website programs.

The Web Site Wizard

The quickest way to create a website in Publisher is to use the Web Site Wizard and let Publisher do most of the design work for you. After you've used the Wizard, you can still modify the design as described later in this chapter.

Starting the Web Site Wizard

| Pull down the File menu and click New.

2 Click Web Sites.

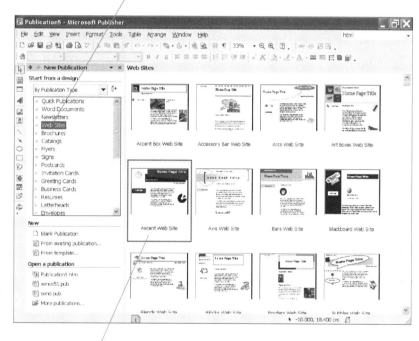

3 Click a design. You can choose interesting single- or multi-page designs for business, community or personal use. Publisher's web graphics are designed for downloading quickly: an important feature!

4 Optional – apply a new formatting/design feature.

To download clip art and photos from the Microsoft Design Gallery Live website, click the Clips Online link in the Insert Clip Art Task Pane.

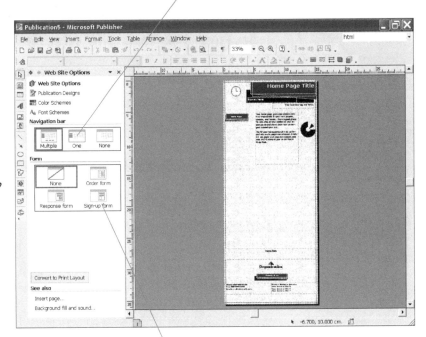

5 Optional – apply a new formatting/design feature.

6 Enter your own text and/or graphics.

To assist you in choosing graphics to include on your web pages, Microsoft has developed hundreds of pictures in the Clip Organizer which are especially 'tuned' for use in web pages. Some are animated to provide an added element of interest to your web pages. Sound clips too are available and can provide the finishing touch to help create a really stunning publication.

Also, by clicking the Design Gallery Object button on the Objects toolbar, you can see a range of email buttons, navigation bars and page dividers which you can include on your web pages. To learn more about the Design Gallery, see Chapter 10.

Creating web pages your way

Although Publisher provides a wide range of predesigned web templates, you may prefer to create your own website from scratch.

Creating a web page manually

1 Pull down the File menu and click New.

2 In the Task Pane, click Blank Publication.

3 In the File menu, click Page Setup.

4 In the dialog, select the Layout tab. Under Publication type, select Web page. Click OK.

5 Add the desired text, pictures, tables, WordArt or other objects (see also below).

A hyperlink is like a key providing access to another part of the web. When you click on a hyperlink, you immediately move to where the link is pointing.

Adding hyperlinks

You can also add a variety of web-specific objects, including hyperlinks. You can create a hyperlink to another part of the same document, another web document, or another part of the web. And your hyperlink can be highlighted text, a selected object, or part of a selected object.

To create a hyperlink from an object, first select the object you want to change to a hyperlink. Next, click the Hyperlink command in the Insert menu. Then carry out the following steps:

Instead of using the Hyperlink command in the Insert menu, you can click the Hyperlink button on the Standard toolbar:

1 Select the object or text you want to serve as a hyperlink.

2 Press Ctrl+K.

3 In the Link to section of the Insert Hyperlink dialog, select a hyperlink type.

4 On the right of the dialog, select/enter an item to link to then click OK.

To create a hyperlink from a part of a selected object, first click the Hot Spot *button:*

on the Objects toolbar. Then use the Insert Hyperlink dialog box to choose your desired link options as described on the previous page. Finally, Publisher inserts an AutoShape as a hyperlink. Drag this to the correct location and resize it appropriately.

Use the procedures here to change an existing background, if required.

The Background command in the Format menu is available only when working with web pages.

Including a textured or coloured background

Complementary colours and textures can create depth and stimulate added interest in your website. Publisher provides a range of textures and colours which you can apply to your web pages.

Adding a background

| Choose Background in the Format menu.

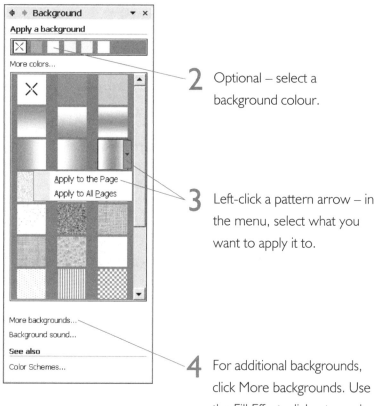

2 Optional – select a background colour.

3 Left-click a pattern arrow – in the menu, select what you want to apply it to.

4 For additional backgrounds, click More backgrounds. Use the Fill Effects dialog to apply a more specialised fill.

Including animated graphics

Publisher converts any rotated text, BorderArt, and gradient text fills used in text frames to graphics, which will not load as quickly as 'pure' text.

If the background colour/texture is too strong, reading web text may be difficult for your readers, and can detract from the main points of your message. Create adequate contrast between text and background.

Use the standard techniques (Insert, Picture, Clip Art or Insert, Picture, From File) to add pictures to your web pages.

Web browsers display plain text more quickly than pictures. If you expect most of your users may not have fast PCs, consider limiting the size, number and type of pictures or animations you use.

Animated graphics – also known as animated GIFs – used in web pages are typically smaller icon-type images that contain some moving components. An animated graphic can enhance interest in a web page and provide an effective eye-catching focus.

Including an animated picture in your web page

1 Insert Publisher CD-ROM number 2 (marked Media Content) in your drive.

2 Open the Insert menu and choose Picture, From File.

3 Go to the FILES/PFILES/MSOFFICE/ MEDIA/CNTCD1/ANIMATED folder.

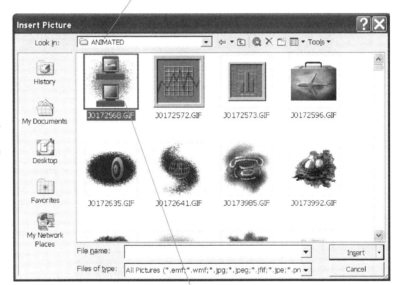

4 Double-click an animation.

Once the animation is placed on the page, you can resize or move it just like any other object. You can view any animated pictures you place on a web using the Web Page Preview command (but animations don't run in Publisher itself) – see page 185.

Adding sound content

You can include sound as a background component so that when visitors view your page, the desired sound clip plays automatically. Sound components can be made up of music, speech, other miscellaneous sounds or a combination of any of these.

Once you've placed your chosen sound component on the page, you can't hear it in Publisher: instead, listen to it in your browser when you preview it (providing your PC hardware supports sound) – see page 185.

Including a background sound component

1 On the Tools menu, click Options.

2 In the Options dialog, select the General tab and click the Web Options button.

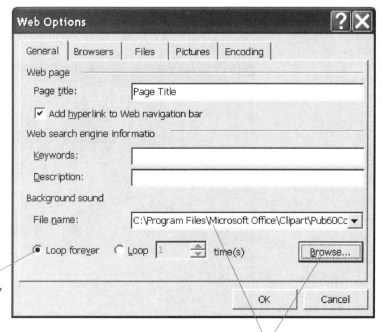

Specify whether you want the sound to 'loop' (play continuously).

3 Specify a sound (or click Browse and choose one in the dialog).

4 Click OK twice.

Creating an online form

A web page form is the electronic equivalent of a paper-based form. But a web form can be much more valuable. Web forms are an ideal addition to a website if you want to gain important information and make the job of submitting this information easy for your visitors. In fact, a key point about designing a web form is that it should be quick and easy for your visitors to complete – if it's not, unless you offer some compelling reason to stick with it, the chances are your visitors won't bother to complete it.

What makes up a web form

Publisher provides the following seven types of component that can be used to make up a form:

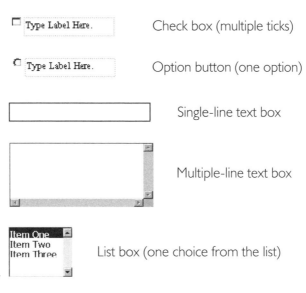

Creating a form: your two choices

You can use one of the predesigned forms in the Design Gallery. Publisher provides three basic designs: an Order form, a Response form and a Sign-up form. You might need to modify the chosen form to meet with your precise requirements, although this is easy to do. Alternatively, you can design and create a form entirely from scratch.

You can create a form from scratch using the Form Control button on the Objects toolbar:

Click this button to display a floating menu containing access to the components listed. Click your desired component (for Submit or Reset, also complete the dialog); Publisher places it on the page. Finally, fine-tune the placement and labelling of each component used.

Using Publisher's predesigned web forms

1 On the Objects toolbar, click the Design Gallery button:

2 Click the Objects by Category tab.

4 Double-click a form.

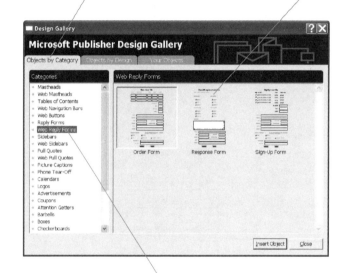

3 Select Web Reply Forms.

When you position a form object on the page, make sure the form doesn't touch other objects on the page. If other objects overlap onto the form, the form controls may not function properly. Ideally allow a clear area of free space around a web form.

The most important part: dealing with your data

Now you can decide how you want to collect the data your web form collects. You can see the options available by double-clicking the Submit button: Publisher then displays the Command Button Properties dialog box. Click Form Properties. Three options are then available:

• Save the form data in a file stored on the web server.

• Have the form data sent to you by email.

• Collect the form data using a program from your Internet Service Provider (ISP).

Discuss your best option with your Internet Service Provider as processing form data can be tricky to set up.

Adding text descriptions to graphics

Even nowadays, more people than you might think do not view web graphics. These include people who have:

Note that text descriptors also display in the following situations:

• When pictures are missing from a website.

• When they're still in the process of loading.

- Text-only browsers.

- Disabled their graphics display.

- Voice readers.

- Very slow Internet connection speeds.

As a result, it's a good idea to apply text descriptors to web graphics. Descriptors provide a pithy definition.

Applying a text descriptor

You can't apply descriptors to animations.

1 Select the relevant picture.

2 Pull down the Format menu and click Picture.

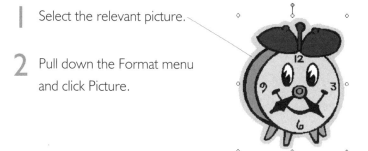

3 Select the Web tab.

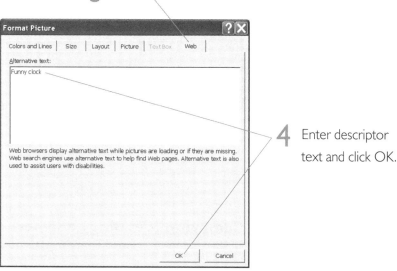

4 Enter descriptor text and click OK.

Changing your website's design

Text hyperlinks are easily spotted. Publisher displays each hyperlink in blue and underlines it.

Creating web pages is an evolutionary process. Rarely will you design a page first time without having any desire to experiment with, or change completely, its look: the business of design involves emotions, 'feel' and creativity, which can vary often. Sometimes you may also want to change the address to which a hyperlink points. Remember, you can do this for a text hyperlink or an object hyperlink.

Changing the address of a text/object hyperlink

It's a good idea to keep a backup copy of your website files, before changing the originals.

1 Select the hyperlink you want to change.

2 Click the Hyperlink command in the Insert menu.

3 Choose one of four ways to change the location to where a hyperlink points.

Re step 4 – the options available depend on which location you selected in step 3.

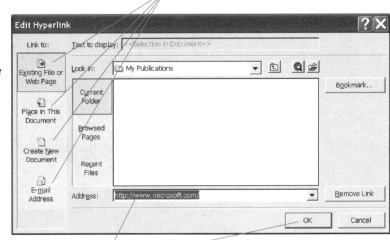

Here's a quick way to check if an object or a piece of text is a hyperlink and if so, where it points to. Simply place the mouse pointer on top of the text or object you want to check. Publisher then displays a ScreenTip with details of the hyperlink (if applicable):

http://www.microsoft.com/

4 Enter the new address or page to which you want the hyperlink to point, then click OK.

Removing (deleting) a hyperlink

In the dialog box above, click the Remove Link button.

Web publishing – an overview

Preliminaries

You can save publications (as HTML files) to network, web or FTP servers. You can do this if you've created a shortcut to the appropriate folder. This is possible because Microsoft has redefined its HTML format.

HTML enhancements

The standard web format (*.html or *.htm) incorporates the following:

You can send web pages as email attachments (or HTML content) directly from within Publisher 2002. Follow the procedures on page 168.

- It's a Companion File format (Microsoft regards it as occupying the same status as its proprietary formats); this means that you can create/share rich web documents with the Publisher 2002 tools used to create printed documents

- It duplicates the functionality of the proprietary formats (i.e. all the usual Publisher 2002 features are preserved when saving in HTML format)

- It's recognised by the Windows Clipboard. This means that data can be copied from Internet Explorer and pasted directly into Publisher 2002

So far, we've discussed adding and changing only those elements which are in some way related to the web. All other non web-specific items in your web pages like pictures, tables, WordArt, text, shapes, etc., are treated by Publisher in the same way as any paper-based document, and so will not be repeated here.

HTML output viewed in a browser (see page 185) – the clock is an animated graphic

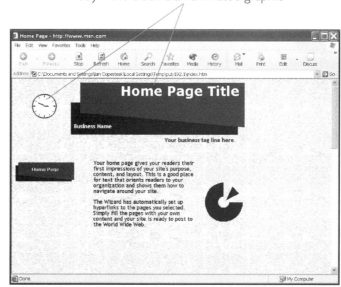

Creating shortcuts

To create a shortcut to a web/FTP folder, you must have the following:

- *a live Internet connection*
- *rights to view/save files*
- *its URL*

To create a shortcut to an intranet folder, you must have the following:

- *a network connection*
- *rights to view/save files*
- *its network address*

To create a web folder, first get details of servers which support web folders from your:

- *system administrator*

or

- *Internet Service Provider*

Re step 2 – users of Windows NT 4 or 98 should click Web Folders instead. In step 3, double-click Add Web Folder and complete the wizard.

In order to save web-format documents to network, web or FTP servers, you need to have created a shortcut to the relevant folder.

Creating shortcuts to web/FTP folders

1 Open the Open (File, Open) or Save As... (File, Save As) dialog and do the following:

3 Double-click Add Network Place.

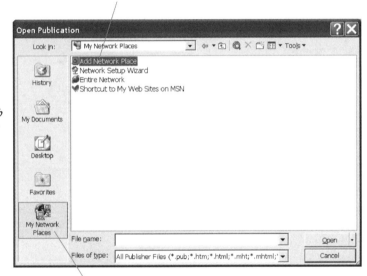

2 In Windows 2000, Me or XP, click here.

4 Follow the on-screen instructions

Creating shortcuts to local network folders

This requires a different procedure.

Windows 2000/Me/XP users should use My Network Places, while Windows NT 4.0 and 98 users should use Network Neighborhood. (For how to do this, see your system administrator.)

Publishing to the web

Previewing your work before saving

Pull down the File menu and do the following:

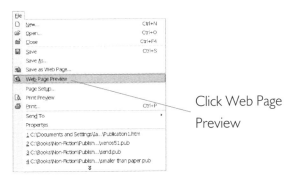

Click Web Page Preview

Before you can save files to web folders or FTP sites, you must first have carried out the relevant procedures. See the facing page.

Your browser now launches, with your work displayed in it. To close it when you've finished using it, press Alt+F4.

Publishing publications – the quick route

Pull down the File menu and click Save as Web Page. Then do the following:

Re step 1 – carry out one of the following procedures according to which version of Windows you're running:

- *Windows NT 4 and 98 users – use Network Neighborhood to save to a local network folder and Web Folders to save to a web or FTP folder*

- *Windows 2000, Me and XP users – use My Network Places to save to a local network folder or to a web or FTP folder*

1 Click here. In the list, select a recipient (see the HOT TIP).

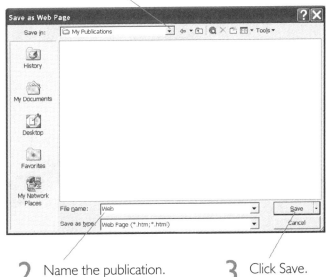

2 Name the publication.

3 Click Save.

Editing in Internet Explorer

When you create HTML files from within Publisher 2002 (see below), they can be edited from within Internet Explorer (version 5 or later).

Look at the illustration below:

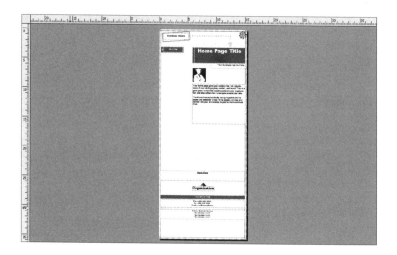

This is a Publisher web page. You can use the techniques discussed on page 185 to convert it to a HTML file. Once the HTML file has been opened in Internet Explorer, do the following:

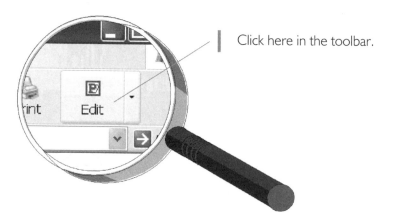

Click here in the toolbar.

2 The HTML file opens for editing in Publisher 2002, with the formatting intact.

Index

Internet Explorer
    Editing publications in   186
Intranets
    Saving publications to   183

Kerning
    Applying to text   75
Keywords
    Adding to clips   117
    Amending in clips   117
    Removing from clips   117

Labels
    Creating   94
Language
    Specifying for text   153
Layout guides
    Setting   143
    Snapping to   144
Lines
    Drawing   46
Linking/embedding objects   43–44
Logo Designs Task Pane   88, 131
Logos
    Creating   131

Mail merge
    Aborting   96
    Address list
        Creating   92
        Editing   92
        Filtering   93
        Selecting   93
        Sorting   93
    Placeholders
        Inserting   94
        Previewing   95

Printing   96
Master page   28, 38, 147
    Activating   12
    Adding headers/footers   145–146
    Placing watermarks on   131
Mastheads   132
Measurement toolbar   48
Measurement units   14
Menu bar   11
Microsoft Office compatibility   9
Microsoft Word
    Editing in   57

New Publication Task Pane   94
Non-printing workspace area   11
Numbered lists
    Creating   79

Object Linking and Embedding   43–44
Object position indicator   11, 14
Object size indicator   11, 14
Object stack
    Defined   38
Objects
    Adding to tables   109
    Aligning   35
    Aligning on the page   34
    Bordering   39, 51
    Changing fills   52
    Changing patterns   53
    Copying   68
    Embedding   43
    Flipping   36
    Grouping   37
    Hiding part of   48
    Introducing   24
    Layering on a stack   38
    Linking   43–44
    Making 3D   54
    Making opaque   41
    Making transparent   40
    Moving   33
    Nudging   35
    Positioning precisely   35
    Recolouring in tables   107
    Resizing   34

P

R